HOMESCHOOLING FROM A TO Z

Principles For Successful Homeschooling

Carolyn Tatem

FOREVER
publishing

FOREVER PUBLISHING, LLC

Homeschooling from A to Z, (Principles for Successful Homeschooling)

Copyright@2020 by Carolyn Tatem

All rights reserved. No part of this publication may be reproduced, stored in a retrieval system, or transmitted in any form or by any means-- electronic, photocopy recording or otherwise without the prior written permission of the publisher. The only exception is brief quotations in printed reviews.

Library of Congress Control Number: 2020914721

ISBN: 978-0-9962851-9-3

Scripture taken from the New King James Version. Copyright 2017 and 1982 by Thomas Nelson. Used by permission. All rights reserved.

Cover design by AugustPride, LLC
Interior design and layout by Rick Soldin

Printed in the United States of America

I dedicate this book to my family for believing in me. It is because they believed that I could, that I did. First, I thank God for ordering the steps of my family and making a way for me to homeschool. Second, I thank my husband of 22 years, William Tatem for encouraging me to try homeschooling. Also, for his courage to be the main provider for our household. He wasn't afraid of the challenge and what it would mean for our family. His famous words were, "try it!" If it doesn't work for our children, they can go back to a traditional school. Third, I thank my children Ciara and Ahmad for asking the question, "Mom, why can't you homeschool us?" I love you!

Lastly, I want to dedicate this book to my beautiful grandmother, Delores D. Lucas who passed on Tuesday, September 1, 2020, while I was in the midst of publishing this book. Thank you for all of the home training you gave me and my children.

Contents

Foreword	vii
Introduction	ix

1   The *A* Principles 1
       • Attitude • Acceptance • Accountability • Attendance

2   The *B* Principles 7
       • Balance • Boys • Bible • Banking

3   The *C* Principles 13
       • Confidence • Curriculum • Church • Customizable

4   The *D* Principles 19
       • Dates • Determination • Dress Attire • Discipline

5   The *E* Principles 25
       • Education • Elementary • Engage • Excellence

6   The *F* Principles 29
       • Family • Finances • Focus • Fun

7   The *G* Principles 37
       • Girls • Goals • Grades • Gratitude

8   The *H* Principles 43
       • Home • High School • Homeschooling • Help

9   The *I* Principles 49
       • Independence • Information • Inner Circle • Image

10   The *J* Principles 55
       • Job • Joy • Joining Each Other • Juggle

11   The *K* Principles 59
       • Keeper • Kindergarten • Kids • Kitchen

12   The *L* Principles 65
       • Love • Learning Styles • Legal • Library

13 The *M* Principles. 71
• Manage • Memories • Movies • Music

14 The *N* Principles. 75
• Neatly • Negativity • News • No

15 The *O* Principles. 81
• One On One • Options • Opportunities • Overwhelming

16 The *P* Principles. 85
• Parents • People • Portfolio • Planning

17 The *Q* Principles. 91
• Qualified • Quiet Time • Quitting • Quality Time

18 The *R* Principles. 95
• Reading • Record Keeping • Respect • Review

19 The *S* Principles. 101
• Schedule • Socialization • Sports • State Supervision

20 The *T* Principles. 109
• Technology • Testing • Transcript • Travel

21 The *U* Principles. 115
• Umbrella • Understanding • Underestimate • University

22 The *V* Principles. 121
• Vacation • Validate • Variety • Vocabulary

23 The *W* Principles 127
• Why? • Work • Worry • Writing

24 The *X, Y,* & Z Principles 133
• X-Ray • The "Y" Principle You • The "Z" Principle Zebra

Closing 138

About the Author 139

Foreword

by: Ciara Tatem

"Homeschooling from A to Z" is great for all moms and dads who are interested or want to know more about homeschooling their children. I, myself, was homeschooled from middle through high school so I know first-hand the journey of homeschooling. Since my mom was already a teacher before deciding to homeschool many would say that she was prepared and fully equipped for the task. Though that might have given her some peace and understanding of how things should go, homeschooling her own children and being responsible for our education was a different experience. I knew that she had my best interests at heart and would do everything in her power to make sure I was prepared for the next step.

I remember at the end of our first year of homeschooling we didn't get the review from the homeschooling coordinator we were expecting. My brother and I had to work through the summer to complete more work. After that year, we worked hard to make sure that was never the case again. I enjoyed how flexible homeschooling could be and learning independently. In this book, my mom answers a lot of the questions I have been asked so many times:

"Do you wear your pajamas all day?,"
"Do you have homework and tests?,"
"Are you really learning anything?"

She is transparent about our journey and how we made it to my high school graduation. While I don't believe homeschooling is for every child or family, I believe it can be done successfully and effectively.

Homeschooling from A to Z can be read from cover to cover or as a reference book used to guide you along the way.

Introduction

I NEVER DREAMED THAT I WOULD HOMESCHOOL MY CHILDREN! Children are gifts from God and you only get one chance to raise them. As parents you have your child's best interests at heart. You're their biggest cheerleader and because of that, you can homeschool your child!

Homeschooling is an opportunity to focus on educating your own child, teaching your children the things that you really want them to know and the basic things that every child should know. Homeschooling full time may not be for everyone but certainly all good parents should be educating their children in the home in some way.

I started homeschooling because both of my children asked me to try it. There were no special needs or behavior issues. My daughter had just completed the 5th grade in a traditional school and my son had completed the 2nd grade. My original goal was to just get my daughter through middle school and to homeschool my son along with her. I ended up homeschooling my daughter from 6th grade through high school. I never thought I would go that far. I homeschooled my son from 3rd through 5th grade.

Due to Covid-19, many parents were forced to homeschool. For the first time in years, parents had to spend time educating their children and overseeing their child's education online. Some embraced this and others had a difficult time for various reasons. Many were caught by surprise and were clueless about how to begin homeschooling.

It doesn't matter if you are homeschooling temporarily or planning to homeschool permanently, Homeschooling from A to Z will provide you with principles to help you start and maintain successful homeschooling.

Chapter One
THE A PRINCIPLES

Attitude

Homeschooling! "Why would anyone want to do that? It's easier to just send your children to school." This was my original attitude towards homeschooling. You see, I am an educator and I was very happy with being in a classroom teaching other people's children. I believe that they learn so much by being in a classroom with others, good and bad. Therefore, it took me a while to decide to homeschool. My original attitude was negative. I didn't think it could be done well, and I wasn't sure that I could successfully educate my children.

Your attitude determines your altitude. Your attitude is your disposition and feelings towards homeschooling. If you don't take it seriously then you will not be serious about putting in the necessary time, discipline and work that is required to be successful. Your altitude refers to the extent or distance upward. Therefore, if you have a good attitude towards homeschooling, you and your child can reach high heights. It is so important to have a positive attitude and to see homeschooling as a privilege because not everyone can homeschool.

In addition to having a positive attitude, you need to realize the seriousness of educating your child. In order to homeschool permanently, you have to withdraw your child from the traditional educational system and come up with a plan to do education at home. This is serious business because you become responsible for educating your child.

The key to having a good attitude is to keep putting good information in your mind and your thoughts. Also, you should surround yourself with people who are homeschooling or who have successfully completed their homeschool journey. When you see that it can be done and done successfully, it is very encouraging. You will need to encourage yourself on a regular basis. You must tell yourself things like: "I can do this, I want to do everything that I can to help my child succeed, I may not know everything but God is going to provide everything that I need to successfully homeschool." He will put the right people in place to help you on this journey.

Since homeschooling is a different educational path, I have had many days where I questioned myself. "Why are we doing this? I could simply enroll my children back into a traditional school setting." There is an easier way; why am I choosing the more challenging way? Not only have I questioned myself but there are other people who will come along and question your decision to homeschool. Some people have a negative attitude towards homeschooling because they really don't know much about it. They have an idea of what they think homeschooling is and usually it's not a positive view. Some will even volunteer to share their negative views with you. If you are not confident and walking with a positive attitude, you will be discouraged. I can honestly say that there have been many days where I have questioned and doubted my ability to homeschool successfully but each time, God would send someone or do something to let me know that this was the path that He wanted for our family. Be encouraged to have a good attitude and to keep believing God for a successful journey. Speak positively each day and don't give up. Remember; your attitude does determine your altitude!

Acceptance

ALTHOUGH MORE PEOPLE ARE CHOOSING TO HOMESCHOOL TODAY, not everyone accepts the idea. I can remember when I first made the decision and started telling a few people. The expression on some people's faces was enough to let me know that they did not like the idea. A few even came out and said, "Why would you want to do that?" I specifically remember someone telling me, "I pay taxes so that my children can go to the public school, so I wouldn't be caught homeschooling." Sometimes it may be your "friends," your children's "friends" and other times it could be family. I never thought I would get flak from people, but then I realized I didn't need to broadcast it to everyone. I got tired of hearing people's negative comments although every now and then I got some positive comments too. Nevertheless, you should be convinced that homeschooling is what you are determined to do. Once you decide to take the homeschooling journey, you need to stick to it regardless of the naysayers.

Everyone does not accept the idea of homeschooling because oftentimes, they don't understand how you can homeschool successfully. People often think the worst. They think your child/children will be lacking social time or something else. They also think that your child couldn't possibly be learning everything that they need by being homeschooled.

I had no idea that my daughter was receiving so much flak throughout her homeschool years until she got ready to apply for college and wrote her college essay. She talked about her homeschooling years and how challenging it was as far as dealing with people. Instead of saying something to me, some people would approach my children and have questions for them. The questions always seemed to be interrogating. "So, what are you learning or what did you do today?" My daughter told me that sometimes she would meet other children who would have something negative to say about homeschool. Some would even make comments like; "I would not want to be around my mother all day." Hearing these negative comments made my daughter uncomfortable with sharing that she was homeschooled when she was younger. As the years went by, she was older and became more comfortable with saying; "I'm homeschooled." Remember; everyone is not going to accept your decision to homeschool. You must make the decision to homeschool, go forward and be encouraged!

Accountability

WHEN I REALLY WANT TO ACCOMPLISH A GOAL, I seek accountability. There is something about sharing with someone who will encourage you and hold you to what you say you are going to do. Most of the goals that I have successfully accomplished have been because I had some form of accountability. In the areas of reading, writing, exercise and weight management, I have had a person to hold me accountable.

I have friends who were homeschooling, and they would check to see how we were doing. I highly recommend connecting with someone or an organization that will hold you accountable. Without accountability, I know that I am likely to slack off, and I never wanted to slack off with my children's education. Some parents choose to connect with a representative from the state that they live in. A representative from the homeschooling office can come to meet with you and your children as a form of accountability also to make sure that you are doing what you are supposed to be doing. I chose to sign up under a Homeschool Umbrella as a form of accountability. I will share more about homeschool umbrellas in the U Chapter.

Having accountability means having someone that you will report to specifically in reference to homeschooling. Your child's education is very important, so you want to make sure that you are giving them your best. You should make sure that your children are learning on a consistent basis and that you have documentation to prove that they are learning. You should be able to explain your homeschooling schedule and how you go about educating your children. When you homeschool, you are responsible for your child's education and you want to successfully get the job done. There are so many things that you may not have thought about so having accountability is great.

Attendance

ALTHOUGH THERE IS A LOT OF FLEXIBILITY WITH HOMESCHOOLING, attendance is very important. You have to make sure that your child is being educated on a consistent basis. This means there should be dedicated time specifically for learning and educating your children. It is so important to have a daily schedule and routine for you and your child. Map out what should be done each day and the amount of time that will be allocated for learning. Be sure that you stick to the schedule so that your child can get enough work completed in each subject. As a parent, it is important you are present to oversee, give feedback, check schoolwork and to encourage your homeschooler along the way.

I kept an attendance book that documented the days that we had school. I also would write down what we focused on each day and record anything that was graded. Keeping good records of their attendance is key. Each state has a certain number of days that students should be in school; you should know the number of days and be sure to comply. If you have a review with the state or a homeschooling umbrella, you may be asked the number of days your kids have had school.

Consistency in attendance is important because it helps your children to develop a daily routine. When you consistently get up, get them ready to learn and work with them, they develop the discipline that will carry them through their years of being educated. As homeschooling parents, we must remember that if we don't show up, our kids don't get educated. We are responsible for educating our children. Good attendance in homeschooling is just as important as good attendance in any other school. You must show up to start the learning process!

Chapter Two

THE B PRINCIPLES

Balance

WHENEVER I THINK ABOUT THE WORD BALANCE, I THINK ABOUT A BALANCE scale that is normally used to symbolize justice and law. The scale swings from one side to the next based on the side that has the heavier weight. I visualize this scale and used to think that balance is giving everything an equal amount of time every day. However, one day I heard someone teach on balance and they explained that balance is about praying and asking God what your focus for the day needs to be. Based on who or what needs more time and attention, that's how you should plan to balance while homeschooling.

If you have more than one child, you will need to balance your time and attention for each child. For example, if you have three children, each child will have daily work but you may divide your time to give each one-on-one time as needed. Some children may require more time than others. You will need to evaluate the age, needs and the ability of each child to determine how much time you need to designate. Balance is necessary when you have one child or multiple children; each child needs one-on-one time with the teacher. If you have an older child, they may be able to help you with the younger children. However, you would need to be mindful of your older child's time if they have work to do too.

Balance is also necessary if you are working from home and homeschooling. No matter how many children you have, you will need to designate time for your work, your child's education, household duties, etc. Each responsibility needs a given amount of time. If you don't learn to balance, too much time will be spent in one area and not enough in other areas.

As a wife, mother, daughter, teacher, and leader in my church, I really had to balance my time between homeschooling and all of my other duties. Although we homeschooled Monday through Friday each week that school was in session, on most weeks there were other things happening in our family which required me to spread myself in other areas. I had to realize that life happens in the midst of homeschooling. Therefore, there will be days when your children may not be taught from their school curriculum or lesson, the lesson may be more on life and what is happening at the moment. It is okay to have a day like this every now and then but again there must be balance. You are responsible for making sure that your child is taught in all the other areas so there must be balance to ensure that your child learns and gets their work done.

Although balance was a challenge on some days, it worked out because in many cases, I had support. Having a spouse, family members, and friends who can help you to get things done can make balancing a lot easier.

Boys

BOYS WILL BE BOYS! One of the things that I certainly observed while homeschooling is how boys truly are different from girls. Their needs are different just as each child is different. I homeschooled my son Ahmad from the 3rd – 5th grade (3 years). I believe he was more of a social learner and needed to be around more people to thrive! One of the things that I enjoyed is being able to tailor my children's education to meet their individual needs and to build upon their natural interest. Ahmad expressed an interest in various things that we were able to explore. He liked drawing, creating art figures, football and even expressed an interest in cooking. He was able to draw and go online for instructions on how to make the figures. For football, we connected with Maryland Park and Planning for flag football and when he was older, he joined a private football team. Playing football while homeschooling provided a nice outlet and so many lessons for my son. He was able to be a part of a team, travel and develop good sportsmanship skills. He enjoyed playing football so much that he ended up playing throughout high school.

We were also able to incorporate cooking in our weekly homeschooling time. You would be surprised by how you can make lessons out of your everyday living. First, he learned to use a measuring cup and sometimes had to calculate the amount of ingredients that something needed (math). Second, he created a recipe book and wrote down various recipes and ingredients. The goal was to write neatly and clearly. Also, he needed to be sure that he included all of the necessary ingredients and steps (reading and writing). Third, we would take a picture of whatever he made and placed it in his recipe book (photography). The time that we spent in the kitchen paid off because my son can now cook for himself and for the family. I love knowing that my son can cook, and I really love when he prepares something to eat for me.

Academically, Ahmad did very well. Each year we would have my son and daughter tested with standardized tests. Ahmad's scores were always good and that let us know that he was learning and doing very well. However, as Ahmad got older, there were days where homeschooling was really a challenge. I think the challenge was accepting the fact that I was his teacher and his mother. He was so used to separating the two. As a result, he and I would always seem to have disagreements about one thing or another. There was definitely some friction. My husband/Ahmad's father had to be the principal and step in. Having a man present to help me raise our son was a big help. I remember him telling Ahmad that he had to learn to respect me as his teacher and that if he refused to do that, he was going back into a regular school environment. After 3 years of homeschooling Ahmad, he made a request to go back to his former school, a private school that at the time, went up to 6th grade. He had friends who were there and he wanted to participate in the 6th grade graduation. We prayed about this decision because it required money that we did not have at the time. God made a way for him to return for the 6th grade, and he was very happy. The school ended up extending the grades to 8th grade, and Ahmad continued his education there until it was time to go to high school. When it was time for high school, we visited several schools to find a good fit. He tested to get into the school of his choice and was accepted. Ahmad entered high school, did well academically, got involved with the choir and played football throughout all his years. He had a wonderful high school experience and graduated on the honor roll. He is now on his way to college. I am not sure if he will ever admit it, but I believe the three years of homeschooling enriched his life and gave him a stronger start.

Bible

THE B.I.B.L.E., YES! THAT'S THE BOOK FOR ME! The Bible is defined as; "Basic Instructions Before Leaving Earth." Although we had plenty of curriculum for various subjects, we made reading the Bible a priority. I explained that it was God's word and He wants to speak to us every day. The Bible was always the first subject that we started with. One of my goals was to teach them to put God first and everything else would truly fall into place. In our beginning years, the three of us would read from the Bible and then discuss. Later, we purchased a curriculum that included the Bible and my children began to study the Bible separately. Together I would teach them basic facts about the Bible like how many books are in the Bible and the names of the books of the Bible. We made up a song to memorize each book of the Bible. It was great to incorporate music into our learning. Singing the books of the Bible song made learning the books of the Bible easier.

Teaching children to develop a habit of reading from their Bible is a major life lesson. I wanted to instill the fact that we need to hear from God's word every day. This is a discipline that I didn't expect for someone else to teach my child. In addition to us learning from the Bible, they would occasionally go to Youth Bible Study at our church. With each lesson learned, we would discuss how God wants us to apply the Word of God to our daily lives.

Bible reading is important to me, so I wanted to make sure that I instilled this in my children. Maybe it's not a priority for you but as a homeschooling parent, you are able to instill your values and priorities in your children on a day to day basis.

Banking

INTRODUCING MY KIDS TO BANKING AT AN EARLY AGE was one of the best things that I could have done. We made banking a part of our homeschooling and incorporated regular trips to the bank. I wanted them to learn about money and the significance of being a good steward over whatever God places in their hands. I took them both to the bank and established savings accounts. We talked about the difference between making deposits and withdrawals. They had to use their math skills to add and subtract. Before we went into the bank we would talk about their transaction and I would go into the bank and have a seat. I taught them how to communicate their needs to the teller and to go up to the counter and handle their own banking needs. The tellers would smile and often give them a lollipop.

For each birthday, they would get money from various friends and family. They would also earn money from doing their chores. With whatever money they had, there were 3 things that would be done: 1) Tithe by giving God 10% or more of your earnings. 2) Decide how much you want to save; we would make a special trip to the bank to make a deposit. 3) They were allowed to spend a portion of the money on a need or something that they wanted. As the years went by they both developed the discipline of saving money.

Teaching banking and financial management skills while homeschooling has given both of my children a good start financially. Both are working and have their own money to manage. I believe you should start teaching this at home. Sometimes this is not taught in a traditional school setting and kids never learn how to manage money or how to save.

Chapter Three
THE C PRINCIPLES

Confidence

CONFIDENCE IS DEFINED AS FULL TRUST, BELIEF IN THE POWERS, BELIEF IN oneself and in one's abilities. I can honestly say that when I started homeschooling, I didn't have much confidence in my abilities. However, I was willing to give homeschooling a try. I remember my husband saying, if it doesn't work out, our children could go back into a traditional school.

Originally, I was only planning to homeschool through middle school because I didn't think that I was capable of homeschooling through high school. I knew that higher levels of math and science had to be taught and the thought of that was enough to scare me away from homeschooling through high school. I knew that my strength was not in teaching math and science, so these were my first concerns. As time went on and I learned more about homeschooling, I discovered that I did not have to personally teach every subject. When I learned that some classes could be outsourced, my confidence towards being able to homeschool through high school increased. I told myself; "This is possible!" and I began to see light at the end of the tunnel. You see where there is a will, there is a way!

There are classes online, in the community, at churches and at community colleges that your homeschooler can take advantage of. I also learned that I could hire a tutor who specialized in the area that my child needed. So whatever subject that I needed help teaching, there was help from other sources. I realized there was more than one way to get the job done and that my children didn't have to lack in any subject.

Parents need confidence to get the job done successfully! When parents are confident, they can instill confidence in their home schoolers. Kids need to know that they can succeed in homeschooling and that their parents will help them. There will be many who question your ability to successfully homeschool so it is important that you have confidence and instill it in your children. Have no doubt that you can successfully homeschool your children.

Curriculum

ONE OF THE FIRST THINGS THAT YOU WILL NEED TO DO after you have decided to homeschool is to select a curriculum. The curriculum consists of the books and resources that you will use to teach your child. There are a variety of books especially designed for homeschoolers of all ages and in every subject. It is so important to select a curriculum that is right for you and for your child. You can research various homeschooling curriculum online and see that there is a plethora of homeschooling curricula to choose from, so much that it can be a bit overwhelming. There is a list of things that your child should be learning on every grade level. Each state has a list of things that are required for students to learn in order to graduate from high school. There are various subjects and a certain number of hours that should be spent in each area. One of the things that I love about curriculum is that you can buy curriculum in any subject that you want your homeschooler to learn. In addition to what is required by the state, parents can decide to teach whatever they want their child to learn.

When selecting your curriculum, you should keep in mind the needs of your child. Think about their age and how they learn best. What subjects are they naturally interested in? What type of learners are they? Can they learn the subject by taking the class online? Do they need lots of visuals, music and activity for learning? What subjects do they personally want to learn more about? For example, if your child thinks they want to be a dentist, you can find ways to start teaching them about teeth and everything pertaining to dentistry. Connect with a dentist and take a field trip to a dentist's office. There are lots of things to consider and so many ways to build a curriculum and make learning fun for your child.

I started my research by informally interviewing other homeschooling moms and asking them questions about what worked and didn't work for them and their children. Sometimes we were blessed with books and materials that friends were no longer using. If you decide to homeschool under a homeschooling umbrella and your child will be taking classes, you should find out the curriculum that will be used. When your child takes classes outside of the home you will need to make sure that you purchase the curriculum that will be used for the class. Although your children can take classes outside of the home, they will still be responsible for completing the assignments at home and you will need to be their overseer. It is helpful to purchase a curriculum that has an answer key and good instructions for parents to be able to follow. You want to be able to support your child by making sure that they are completing assignments, checking their work and discussing what they are learning.

Choosing the right curriculum for your child is very important. Reading and knowing how to properly use the curriculum is just as important. Your choice of curriculum can make learning fun and exciting or it can make it boring and turn a student off from a particular subject. Do your research before making your selection. There is nothing more disappointing than ordering a bunch of curricula that you later find out is not right for your child.

Church

I KNOW EVERYONE DOES NOT ATTEND CHURCH HOWEVER, I thank God for my church! Weekly attending a Bible-believing, Bible-teaching church that has various ministries and activities for adults and children of all ages has been one of the greatest blessings to our homeschooling journey. Being an active member of a church that is alive and has so much to offer helped to make our homeschooling journey successful. I realize that we the people are the church, however, when I refer to the church, I am talking about the physical building where my family and I go to worship and assemble with other believers. Going to church has been a very valuable part of my children's education. Teaching children about God and how to have a relationship with Him is one of the most important things that I wanted my children to learn. Attending every week, hearing the word of God preached, listening to the songs that the choir sings and meeting various people from various places has been a learning experience within itself.

In addition to that, let me explain all of the things that our church provided which made a world of difference to our homeschooling experience. First, our church has a homeschooling umbrella. This means that for a reasonable fee you can get support in the form of; counsel, guidance, homeschooling reviews, classes and activities for your child on a weekly basis. Second, our church has various ministries where children can learn and have activities to enhance their homeschooling education. My daughter was an active member of the Dance Ministry and she was able to use her hours of going to dance towards her education. While in the Dance Ministry, she participated in annual Christmas productions, community outreach and special services. She learned so much just by being an active dance member. Third, my daughter was a member of the children's magazine ministry. In this ministry, she wrote various articles in the kid's column. She was able to write using her reading and writing skills in this ministry. In addition, there were times where she would have to interview people for her articles. This was a wonderful learning experience. Fourth, our church provided weekly Bible study and a leadership program for teens. Both of my children participated and benefited from the lessons that were created just for them. The last thing that I would say about the church is that every week I was able to gain strength and encouragement to continue educating my children. Homeschooling is a different route and sometimes I would question myself by asking: "Why am I doing this or am I doing the right thing?" Whenever I would doubt or get discouraged, either the message or someone would encourage me and give me strength for my journey.

Homeschooling my children has allowed me to incorporate church and teach my children about God. This is something that would not be allowed in the traditional school environment. It is important to share and teach your values, beliefs and your faith with your children. Being a part of a good church and having a relationship with God is something that I value and wanted to teach to my children. Think about what you value and what's important to you. How can you make it a part of your child's homeschool journey?

Customizable

ONE OF THE GREATEST THINGS ABOUT HOMESCHOOLING is that it is customizable. This means that parents can build their child's education based on their personal preferences and their child's individual needs. Whatever you would like to include in your child's education can be included. Whenever you customize you should always consider the needs of your homeschooler, their age, their interest, learning styles and what is required. Each state has its requirements with what must be taught for a child to graduate. Therefore, you are responsible for making sure that your child has the required courses completed. You should select a curriculum that will help you to teach your children the required courses. You can select books, classes that are online and resources from various places. Once you have selected a curriculum, you can also customize the way that you will teach it to your child. Depending upon the needs of your child, you should determine how the material will be taught. There are various methods of teaching the necessary information and you will need to decide what will work best for you and your child.

Not only are the subjects customizable but your day-to-day schedule can also be customized. You can decide upon a schedule that will work for you and your children as long as there is enough time to get the necessary work completed. However, if you want to homeschool for four days a week and have Fridays as a day off or a day for fun things like field trips, arts and crafts, etc., or to take a break, you can do it! You will need to plan your four days of work in such a way that your children can get their work done in four days.

Chapter Four
THE D PRINCIPLES

Dates

MAKING SURE THAT THE DATE IS WRITTEN OR TYPED ON EVERY ASSIGNMENT that your child does is very important especially when you are homeschooling. Creating a paper trail of the assignments that your child completes with the date on it is your evidence. As a homeschooling parent, you will have a homeschooling review or evaluation at some point. If you are under a homeschooling umbrella you will have to meet with someone generally at the end of each quarter to present a homeschooling portfolio. The portfolio is a collection of all the work that your child has completed. One of the things that helps to make a homeschooling review successful is being able to present work that has been dated. The dates help to display consistency in the assigned work.

If your children are very young when you start homeschooling, you will need to teach them how to properly write the date. First, you would need to do a lesson on the date and explain each part of it; the day, month and the year. You can develop an entire lesson around the date. Oftentimes the date is written in the top right corner.

If you are homeschooling your children at a young age, it is wise to teach them about writing their names and the current date on every assignment. This is a good practice because it is required in a traditional school setting and it teaches students to identify their work. They should also understand the significance of writing or typing the current date on each of their assignments. When work is not dated, it is very difficult to prove that you and your child have been working consistently and making good use of the time. Each day that school is conducted, there should be dated assignments.

Determination

IF YOU ARE GOING TO SUCCESSFULLY HOMESCHOOL, you must have determination! Having your mind fixed on your reason and your purpose for homeschooling helps. There will be days where you may not feel like homeschooling, but you must be determined. When this happens, you must remind yourself that you are responsible for your child's education. You do not want your child to be slighted in any way especially not as a result of something that you did not do. You will have days where you are not feeling good, but you will need to give your child something to work on and be determined. Their education should not stop because of you. That may sound a little harsh but that's the determined attitude that you need to have in order to get the job done.

There will also be days where someone in the family or someone who doesn't quite get or understand why you are homeschooling may come around and make a negative comment about why you are homeschooling. You must ignore the negative remarks and stay focused on your reasons for homeschooling.

Selecting a different educational route for your child is not easy but once you decide to do it, you must be determined. I did not have all the details, but I knew that I had to keep pressing to see my children through. When I first began preparing to homeschool, I remember shaking in my boots. This means that I was scared, but I was willing to keep going forward afraid. It was definitely a walk of faith but I was determined! Here is what I was determined to do: 1) To do my best and to educate my children successfully. 2) To get up every school day and provide my children with the necessary skills to succeed. 3) To expose my children to things and people that would help on their educational journey and 4) Lastly, to finish strong.

There are so many things that we can accomplish when we simply determine in our hearts and minds that this is what we are going to do and stick to it!

Dress Attire

Is DRESS ATTIRE NECESSARY FOR HOMESCHOOL? Even though we were working from home, we had a dress attire for our homeschool! I know that many could care less about this but making sure that my children and I were well presented was a priority for me. Honestly, I have always been this way, so homeschooling was not going to change this. One of the things that I noticed about many of the homeschool moms that I came across was that they didn't seem to take enough time to care for themselves. I know that it is not easy when you are juggling yourself, your husband, your children, the home and homeschooling. It's easy to let yourself go. Also, as a wife, I have always wanted to first feel good about me and then make myself attractive for my husband. I never wanted him to come home and not be satisfied with the way that I looked or for me to be so busy taking care of everything and everybody else that I neglected myself. When I don't feel good about myself, I have very little to give, and I certainly don't display the attitude that I want my children to have.

Many of the moms that I saw looked like they; barely fixed their hair, didn't care about their outward appearance and rarely fixed themselves up. Perhaps they were doing the best that they could, but this was a turn off to me. My daughter and I both noticed this on many occasions, and she would say; "Mom do you have to look like a "homeschool mom?"" I realized that I wasn't the only person who noticed a certain look in many of the homeschool moms we met. I knew that homeschooling required a big financial sacrifice for my family and for many families. Part of the sacrifice meant living on one income and having a tight budget. A tight budget meant I didn't go shopping for anything for me unless it was something I really needed. I may not have been able to get my hair done as often as I would have liked, but I wanted to make sure that my hair was presentable.

Dressing nicely wasn't something that I only wanted to do when we went out of the house. Each day that we had school I would get the kids up and had them to get themselves dressed. We never did school in the pajamas unless someone was sick or it was pajama day. I wanted them to develop a routine of getting up, brushing their teeth, combing their hair and getting dressed for the day. Some days we would not need to leave the house but we were always dressed and prepared just in case we needed to go out. We didn't just wake up and roll out of bed. Having dress attire was a good way to set the tone for our school day.

Discipline

ONE OF THE KEYS TO RAISING A SUCCESSFUL STUDENT IS DISCIPLINE. Homeschooling provides many opportunities for teaching various disciplines. When you set up your homeschool you should think of the disciplines that you want your child to learn. If they have been accustomed to going to a traditional school before homeschooling, they will already have some disciplines in place. You will need to establish the disciplines that you want them to keep practicing at home. For example; I wanted my children to continue to be disciplined to get up each day, make their bed, wash their face, brush their teeth and get dressed just like they did when they went to a traditional school. I also wanted them to know that school was going to start at 9:00 AM and that every day we had a schedule to follow with goals for the day. One of our goals was to be finished around 2:30 in the afternoon.

Another discipline was that we were going to have a designated area for our homeschool. We discipline ourselves to not have homeschooling books and materials all over the house. We designated a room in the basement to be our school classroom. For the first few years of homeschooling, we went into our basement classroom each day that we had school in the house. On some days the kids took classes outside the home, so we were out and about on those days. If I had an appointment or somewhere to go, I would pack up the kids and always pack something that they could do on the go in the car or something that they could sit and do while we were out. As my daughter got older and in high school, she chose to study in her bedroom or in other areas of the house. We did not use the classroom for the high school years of homeschooling.

The D Principles

A lot of discipline is required for the homeschooling parent to get up each day and teach or to make sure that your homeschooler is learning. There are so many other things that will demand your time such as; life, your marriage, your home, friends, family and for some work outside of the home. However, you must set your priorities and discipline yourself to designate the daily necessary hours for your school. If you say that you are homeschooling and you don't make homeschooling your priority, who will? You must put all of your other responsibilities to the side and stick to educating your child. Discipline is necessary to get the job done.

Another part of disciplining your child is teaching them how to be well behaved and self- controlled. This is a necessary discipline because when you do take your children into public you want to make sure that they know how to conduct themselves. Teach the behavior that you want them to display at home in other words home training and be sure to give rewards or positive reinforcement when they comply. When their behavior is not good you must have consequences in place.

Establishing daily routines and rules that you and your homeschooler will practice on a daily basis will help to establish discipline. Remember that children learn by repetition. However, you want to have good things in place for them to repeat each day so they can develop good habits. Think about the disciplines that you want your child to establish or maybe they already have some disciplines in place that you want to maintain. What are the disciplines?

Chapter Five

THE *E* PRINCIPLES

Education

WHAT IS AN EDUCATION? THE DICTIONARY DEFINES AN EDUCATION AS: "The process of facilitating learning, or the acquisition of knowledge, skills, values, beliefs, and habits." What a privilege it is to be able to educate your own children. You are your child's educator along with all of the other people who will be a part of your child's homeschooling journey. I know it's a big responsibility, but all things are possible. As an educator, you get to find out the skills and the knowledge that your child needs based on the state that you live in and teach it to them. You are not confined to teaching based on their age or grade level; you can teach your children as much as you like. If you are not planning to teach them personally in a particular subject, you get to make arrangements for the information to be taught by someone else or another resource. You also get to instill your own values and beliefs into your children. I loved teaching the Bible to my children and being able to incorporate our Christian beliefs into our homeschooling.

There are various methods that can be used to educate such as: teaching, storytelling, field trips, discussion and training. One of the goals of an education is to nourish the good qualities and to draw out the best in every person. As a homeschooling parent who loves their child and wants the very best for them, you are the best person to nourish them. The more time that you spend with your children, the better you will get to know them. As you get to know them you will see their natural strengths, talents and qualities that can be nourished and developed. Spend time observing your child and think about the things they do well, the things they naturally enjoy and you can begin to see how to shape their homeschooling journey.

Elementary

I MET SOME HOMESCHOOLING MOMS who said that they knew that they were going to homeschool when their children were born. I thought this was great on their part because they started motherhood with a homeschooling mindset. This means that they started homeschooling from preschool into elementary. The elementary years are generally grades 1-5 in a formal school setting. When you know that you are going to homeschool from the beginning, you can prepare and start gathering educational tools and resources to use from preschool to elementary. There is so much that can be taught from the very beginning when you start homeschooling during the elementary years.

As I previously mentioned, I started homeschooling when my children were in elementary school. My son was a 3rd grader and my daughter a 6th grader. One of the blessings and challenges that I encountered with moving from a private traditional school setting to homeschooling is that my children already had an idea of how things were at school. They had a tendency to make reference to the way that their former teacher did things or the way that things went in their former school. I constantly had to reiterate that mommy is your new teacher and you have to learn to do things my way. Teaching something differently was a challenge at first, but they eventually got used to having mommy as the teacher. Children learn to adapt, just like they do when they go to a new grade level and have a new teacher in a traditional school. This is where you will need your determination and discipline. If you establish good disciplines and routines at the elementary level, it will help you in homeschooling on the high school level.

The E Principles

Engage

WHEN PARENTS ARE ENGAGED IN THEIR CHILD'S EDUCATION, students are more likely to succeed. When I first started teaching at a high school, I noticed that the students who were excelling the most were the ones where the parents took time to come to the back-to-school nights, parent- teacher conferences or made phone calls to check on their children. Not only coming to the school but checking on them after school to see that their homework is completed and that they were prepared when they had a test. It doesn't matter which educational journey you select for your child, private, public or homeschooling. If you are engaged in the education process, your children are more likely to succeed.

As a homeschooling parent, you must be engaged in your child's education. You are the primary educator or overseer of your child's educational journey. Being engaged is a necessary ingredient for raising good students. To be engaged means that you are involved in your child's learning process. The more engaged you are, the more you learn about your student and the better you are able to help them to succeed. As you find out your child's strengths and weaknesses your goal should be to engage them in assignments and activities that will help to build or strengthen their skills. If you see a need and you are not able to meet the need, this is when you seek help elsewhere. There are so many resources that can be used to enhance your child's homeschooling journey.

One of the things that I learned after engaging with my two homeschoolers is that my daughter was more of an independent learner. Once she was given instruction, she was self-motivated, took responsibility for her own learning and worked independently to get the job done. On the other hand, my son was more of a social learner, he thrived off being with other students to learn. This is why I didn't homeschool him for as long as I did my daughter.

Excellence

EVERY GOOD PARENT WANTS THEIR CHILD TO EXCEL! Homeschooling is a wonderful opportunity to prepare your child for excellence. As a homeschooling parent, you can be intentional about helping your child to excel in every way. Teaching them to strive for excellence and then helping them to achieve it is very important. I think you have to think about what you want your child to obtain at the beginning of each school year and then do everything possible to help them excel.

I honestly believe that homeschooling my children helped them to excel. They were taught things and exposed to things that they would not have been had they been in a traditional school. I was able to spend time teaching them things that perhaps I would not have taken the time to do if I was working a full-time job and not as engaged in their learning process. Every week I would prepare things for us to do, places to go and people to meet. There are so many things that are available that can enhance a student's learning experience and I wanted to be sure to provide my children with everything that I could. I realized that it wasn't just about me and what I had to offer, it was about me exposing them to other things, people and places. I could not provide excellence in teaching math to my daughter. However, I was able to connect her with an excellent math tutor who helped her through her high school years. Whatever you can't do as a parent does not have to hinder your child; you can connect with people who are excellent in what they do and see if they will help you in teaching your child.

Each of us has gifts and talents and as you homeschool your child you want to tap in to their gifts. As you spend daily time with your child, look for their gifts and talents. Look for ways to enhance their gifts and talents to produce excellence.

Chapter Six
THE *F* PRINCIPLES

Family

It would be so nice to have your entire family on board with your plan to homeschool. However, once you make the decision to homeschool and your spouse is in agreement, you've got to stick to it! The truth of the matter is that other family members may not like the idea. Some will come right out and say it; others may not say it, but they are thinking; "Why would you ever want to homeschool?" Hopefully, they will understand it better by and by.

If you are pulling your children from a traditional school setting you will need to explain your plan to your child or children and get them on board. If your children have been attending traditional schooling and you are taking them out to homeschool, they may not fully embrace the idea of homeschooling at first because there are so many uncertainties. They are uncertain about how this is going to work. If a child has never attended school in a traditional setting, they will have nothing to compare to or have any reason for apprehension. Sometimes children are excited about the idea but because they have experienced a traditional education, they are more concerned about what others may think or say about them being homeschooled. As a parent, you must encourage your children and reassure them that they will be fine.

If you are married, it is most important that you and your spouse are in full agreement because homeschooling will impact your household. There are several decisions that you and your spouse will have to make. Here are a few questions to discuss. Will both parents be homeschooling or just one? In my household, I was the primary homeschool teacher. However, I have met families where the mom is the primary teacher but the dad also teaches the children. For example, let's say that you are strong in reading and writing and your spouse is strong in math and science. If your spouse is willing to participate in the teaching, each parent can teach from their strengths. I have also met families where the dad was the primary teacher. So you will need to decide if there are subjects that you and your spouse will teach or will there just be one of you as the primary teacher. Figure out what will work best for your household. If you are a parent who is the primary teacher, will you be at home full time or will you also work outside of the home? Will you have a business on the side or will you primarily operate off one income? How will this affect your family household?

When you have the support of other family members such as the grandparents, aunties and uncles, this is a blessing to your homeschooling journey. Sometimes you need family members to be available to assist you along the way. You may need an extra set of hands, feet or transportation to help you as you homeschool. Knowing that you have family members who are willing to help you as you do what God is calling you to do makes the homeschool journey pleasant. Having family members that are not in support of your decision can be challenging especially if it's your parents (the grandparents). Once you have made up your mind to homeschool, the last thing that you need are negative comments and a lack of support from the ones that you love. Many are negative because of their lack of knowledge about homeschooling. They haven't seen it done successfully and they have negative thoughts about how it will be done. Many automatically think that your child will lack social skills and that homeschooling will hurt your child. Often, once they start seeing the benefits of you homeschooling, they can better embrace the idea. Some benefits that they often see is that your children are learning, they are smart, they know how to socialize and engage with other people, they are well behaved, you are able to teach them and expose them to things that they would not learn in a traditional school and that a parent can homeschool successfully. When family members start seeing great results of your homeschooling, they will usually get on board.

The F Principles

Finances

HOMESCHOOLING WILL AFFECT YOUR FINANCES! Any school will affect your finances! There are various costs associated with every educational journey. In the traditional schools you may have to pay for lunch, uniforms, school supplies, after care, before care, tutoring, etc. When you decide to homeschool, there are costs associated with homeschooling. I will discuss some of the costs that you will need to consider.

- ★ **Curriculum/Materials** – You will need to select and purchase the books and materials that are needed to teach. Think about all the supplies that you will need to make learning fun and to teach in the various subjects.

- ★ **Classes** – Some courses will not be taught by the parent but can be taken online or in other educational environments. There are places that offer classes to homeschoolers, the community colleges or people who you know that will offer tutoring services. In most cases you will have to pay money, but sometimes you may be able to barter services.

- ★ **Clothing** – You will not need to purchase uniforms or specific items that are needed for traditional schools but you will still need to make sure that your children have proper clothing and in the proper sizes. If your child is participating in a sport, dance, etc., you will need to purchase the proper attire for the sport.

- ★ **Computer** – One of the things that will be essential to your child's homeschooling success is having access to a computer. Purchasing a computer and internet services are essential. Both will be a great tool for your child to learn at home. For those who are homeschooling temporarily, the computer allows your child to get instruction from their traditional school. Teachers use the computer to connect with your children and provide online instruction. As a parent, you only need to oversee this process. Students are able to get online instruction when they have a computer and internet capability.

★ **Covering** – If you decide to be under a homeschooling umbrella there is a fee that will need to be paid. I thank God for having a homeschool covering. The covering provided support, wisdom from experienced homeschooling parents and fun activities to help make the homeschooling journey fun for the children. It was also a form of accountability. Each quarter I was responsible for submitting grades for my children and meeting with a homeschool reviewer from time to time to make sure that we were moving along successfully.

★ **Classroom** – One of the things that I got excited about when we decided to homeschool was fixing up a room in the house as our classroom. I wanted to have a specific room for homeschooling and not be all over the house. I needed to focus and so did my children. Having one dedicated room helped us. We knew when it was time for school, we worked in our classroom and when we were done, we were free to move about in the rest of the house. We purchased a desk for both of my children and a teacher desk for myself to place in our classroom. One day Ciara mentioned that the one thing that she was looking forward to in her private school was using a locker and learning how to use a combination lock. We didn't want homeschooling to kill her dream, so we looked online and found a company that sold individual lockers. One Christmas morning, our kids woke up to a set of lockers and pad locks for each of them. They learned how to use a combination lock and boy oh boy did they have fun with that. They even decorated the lockers. It was a joy to store their books in the lockers and to lock it up in the classroom. The kids were very excited about this.

These are just some of the costs to consider. As I mentioned, there are various costs associated with every educational journey. To be able to homeschool is a blessing. The cost is little or nothing when you think about all that your children will receive and how they will benefit from having a tailor-made education with loving parents who are nourishing and preparing them to be the best human being that they can be. This is priceless!

When our family decided to homeschool, we did not know how we would afford all the things that were needed, but I am a witness that God will provide. Curriculum, clothing, classes and everything that we needed was provided. Oftentimes, we don't see how it will all get done, but a way was made out of no way! It is wise to sit down beforehand and estimate the cost of homeschooling before you begin.

Focus

THERE ARE SO MANY HOMESCHOOLING DAYS that I had to focus on my, "WHY?" When I focused on my "why," which is my reason for homeschooling, I was able to persevere. I had to focus by telling myself that this was my season to homeschool my children and that I was going to do my best to make sure that they were well educated. I have to admit that there were so many days where I didn't feel qualified to be fully responsible for my child's education but because I knew others who had done it successfully, I believed that I could. I knew of moms who homeschooled when they had so much less to work with; today we have so much more.

I was homeschooling in the midst of everything else that was happening in my life, and I had to learn to dedicate 9:00am – 2:30pm to homeschooling my children and put everything else on hold. This means that I would go downstairs into the classroom when it was time to homeschool and shut out the rest of my house, responsibilities, emails and the phone. I tried multi-tasking with other things, but that didn't work. I would get on the phone with someone and talk longer than expected; before I knew it the time for me to teach something was gone. My children needed my undivided time and attention. Therefore, I had to focus on my children during our homeschooling time. You will find that you just can't do everything and be there for everybody while trying to homeschool your children. I would even ask people to call me on my lunch break or after 2:30 in the afternoon. Think about it, in a traditional school setting, when school is in session, teachers are not allowed to take outside calls when they are teaching school. A teacher has to wait until his/her lunch break or until after school to socialize or to handle her personal business. As a good teacher, you must pay attention to the needs of your students, recognize what you need to teach, what they retain and what you need to repeat. If you don't focus, time will slip away from you and you will not get the necessary work done in a timely fashion.

Focus is necessary to successfully homeschool because if you are all over the place it will be hard to get things done. When you lose your focus or you lose your enthusiasm, remind yourself that it is a privilege to be able to homeschool.

Fun

LET'S HAVE SOME FUN! One of my goals along with homeschooling was to make learning fun. I had a vision of going places and doing things that would allow my children to learn and have memorable experiences. I realized that the homeschooling years are memorable years and each time that they learned and had fun, we were creating memories. I spent a lot of time thinking of activities, field trips and things to do that would allow them to learn, enjoy themselves as well as have fun. I strongly believe that when learning is fun, children will want to learn.

I think we had so much fun the first year of homeschooling that we did less book work. When I went for my first-year homeschooling review, I was told that we had not finished enough of the book work. The evaluator recommended that we continue school through the summer to finish more of the book work. I was not happy about this nor were my children. I felt like such a failure. We had a great year and a great time learning and creating memories; however, we had not completed enough of the curriculum. The lesson learned is that you have to have balance. There should be a good mix of hard work, time in the books and some fun time.

One of the lessons that I learned was to document our fun time and when it was possible, we would make our fun time educational. For example, if you plan a trip to California, have your children learn facts about the state of California. Write about some of the significant things that happen there or places to visit in California. Another example is if you go on a shopping trip at your favorite store, depending upon the age of your child you can have them research the company to find out facts about the business or business owner. There are ways for children to learn about everything and have fun at the same time. So much of the information is supplied on the internet.

Some of the things that we did for fun were: roller skating, museums, pottery, plays, gardening, going to the park, going to the playground, going to story time at the library, splash parks, amusement parks, bowling, pumpkin patch, cooking, arts and crafts and movies.

As we were having fun, I learned to take pictures and create videos of us having fun. Pictures are a part of creating memories and can be used to document events for the homeschooling review. Each year we would create photo books and print pictures of the activities, events and field trips that we took. A picture is worth a thousand words, so have fun creating memories throughout your homeschooling years.

Chapter Seven
THE G PRINCIPLES

Girls

When you are homeschooling a girl and a boy you are likely to notice the differences. Although both boys and girls were created equally, they are different; therefore, we should learn what works best for each. According to studies done on educating girls vs boys, girls develop earlier when it comes to their verbal memory storage. There is a region of the brain critical to verbal memory storage called the hippocampus. They say that girls have a larger hippocampus and that it has a profound effect on their vocabulary and writing.

My daughter Ciara was going to the 6th grade when we started homeschooling. She was a great student at her former school and was always concerned about doing well academically. I also noticed that she was more of an introvert. We had a couple of events at the house where her classmates were invited over and although she enjoyed her time with them, she never seemed to request more time with them. Hanging out with a group of girls on the weekend or after school was over never seemed to be a desire for our daughter. Now for my son, it's a different story. I mention this because some people think that homeschooling causes students to be less social. However, Ciara was naturally this way before she began homeschool and my son was naturally the more social one. I believe a child's personality has a lot to do with how well they adjust to homeschooling. This is why it works better for some kids than others. Not that it couldn't work for every child. Some personalities are more challenging than others and would require more activities, interactions and peer involvement.

Although Ciara wasn't big on hanging out or having lots of friends over, she had her share of activities which required her to interact with others. She was an active member of the Dance Ministry at church, The Magazine Ministry for Kids and participated in several Christmas Productions. We also took regular field trips and volunteered at places that required interaction with children and adults. In addition, we regularly had guests in our home that both of my children helped to entertain.

She was easy to homeschool because of her inner drive and self-discipline. Throughout our homeschooling journey she kept me on track with things that needed to be done. In many cases she would initiate her own learning by reading or researching information. Once she was given instruction and curriculum for each subject, she was ready for the week. We would sit down each week and map out what she was going to learn and the assignments that needed to be completed along with deadlines. Ciara was driven enough to complete the assignments with very little supervision.

As a result of the drive that she had, my daughter finished most of her high school requirements early. During her senior year of high school, she was able to spend the year taking college courses at the local community college. The courses that she took counted towards her college degree and gave her a head start. Homeschooling allows a student to move at a pace that is perfect for them. If a child needs more time to complete work that time can easily be provided. On the other hand, if a child is moving at a faster pace and desires to move on, the sky's the limit.

Goals

WHAT ARE YOUR HOMESCHOOLING GOALS? Do you plan to homeschool all the way through or only for a few years? Will you start at the beginning when your children first begin school or will you allow them to go to a traditional school, then homeschool? The choice is yours. Determine what your goals will be and go for it.

My goal was to simply homeschool my kids through middle school, especially my daughter. However, I ended up homeschooling her from 6th grade through high school. This was beyond any of my initial plans. Since my son was only in the 3rd grade when I started homeschooling, my plan was to get him through middle school. However, Ahmad had a different goal and we allowed him to express his desire. His goal was to go back to the school that he started in the first grade and finish middle school with the students that originally started school with him.

My goal as a homeschooling mom was to do the best that I could do for each child. I wanted to be in tune with what God wanted for each one of them. I prayed a lot about the things that God wanted to accomplish on our homeschooling journey. I prayed that I would not miss whatever God wanted to reveal on the journey. My goal was to provide the best education possible. In addition, it was very important to me that both of my children had a relationship with God and learned how to include Him in their daily conversations. My goal was to teach my children something about God on a daily basis.

It is always important to have goals and to know what you are trying to accomplish. Seek God for your goals and take time to hear what He has to say concerning you and your children.

Grades

JUST BECAUSE YOU ARE HOMESCHOOLING DOES NOT MEAN that you do not have to grade assignments. When I use the word "grade" I mean evaluating your child's work. Some do not like using a letter grade such as; A, B, C, D or F. However, you need to have a method of communicating what a student has right and what is wrong. As the teacher, you also need to communicate to your child what is okay and what needs to be corrected. It is so important to grade your child's work on a regular basis, so that you can see how well or how poorly they may be doing. For example, if a child makes a mistake in math and no one grades his or her work, he would never be aware of the mistake and will likely make the same mistake again. Grades help to give students feedback and it encourages them along the way. Also, grades help to give parents and teachers the necessary feedback on how their child/students are doing.

In the younger years like kindergarten, you may be able to get away from traditional grading and try something else like using stickers, incentives, etc. However, the older the students, the more likely you will need to use grades. Grades are important and they can and will be held against you! If your child plans to go to a traditional school at some point or even go to college after being homeschooled, you will need grades. Colleges still like to take a look at your child's transcript. As a homeschooling mom who was reporting to a homeschooling umbrella, I was told to aim for at least one grade per week in each subject. This worked for me. I would pick one paper per week, per subject and grade it. We kept one big notebook and stored the graded work in the notebook.

Both of my children earned good grades as homeschoolers. However, since I homeschooled Ciara longer, she received more grades from me as her primary teacher. I think Ciara thought she was getting A's on most of her work because, "I was just giving her A's ". I don't think that she honestly believed that she was earning A's. Taking classes at other learning institutions allowed Ciara to realize that her work really was excellent. She did not make an A because of me; it was totally the result of her hard work and work ethic. When my daughter took college classes, she continued to earn A's in many of her subjects. Throughout her college years, she made the Dean's list. Good grades can lead to good things like scholarships and internships.

Grades are also necessary for homeschooling/portfolio reviews. When the homeschooling parent has a portfolio review, two of the main things that the reviewer will look for are: 1) Graded work and 2) The date. Each assignment that your child completes should have their names, date and the grade. When the work is graded, the homeschool reviewer can easily see a consistent system of homeschooling.

Gratitude

DO CHILDREN NATURALLY COME INTO THE WORLD WITH GRATITUDE? I would probably answer this question by saying NO. Gratitude is something that has to be taught. I want to encourage every parent to teach their children all about gratitude! I know they are your children and you can teach whatever you would like, but I think you would agree that we all need to know what this word means and practice it. When children first learn to ask for something, most parents start teaching gratitude by training their children to say thank you! This is a good start, but it must not stop there. Having gratitude is so important and when children and adults learn to put it into practice, it can change the course of their lives in a positive way.

Let's talk about the meaning of the word gratitude. The dictionary defines gratitude as "The quality or feeling of being grateful or thankful." Being grateful is being warmly appreciative of someone's kindness and realizing benefits that you have received. You would think that when someone does something for us by expressing acts of kindness or giving something that they don't have to give, we would naturally say thank you. However, this is not the case. If we don't teach our children gratitude, they may not be thoughtful enough to take the time to express their gratitude. Human beings are generally selfish and really have to be trained how to be grateful and how to express their gratitude.

Being grateful and expressing gratitude are two different things. I can say that I am grateful for my parents but never take the time to tell them or do anything to express my gratitude. I really want my children to practice doing both. I want them to always have a mind of gratitude. We start by being grateful to God first; grateful for each day that He allows you to see with breath in your body, food to eat and clothes on your back; the list goes on and on. Then we can think about the people who are in our lives who we need to be grateful for and take time to express our gratitude. One way to put this into practice is to start a gratitude journal. Have your children write about their gratitude in a journal or create a gratitude document on the computer and type out their gratitude each day. It only takes a few minutes, but this is a good way to start or end the day. Adults can participate in journaling their gratitude as well. It is very therapeutic.

One of my desires was to raise children who are grateful and to teach them different ways to express their gratitude. Let's not forget that gratitude must be taught because it is not something that we just automatically know how to express. Teach your children and start by being a good example in the way that you express your gratitude. It doesn't take much time and it often doesn't cost us much, but we must be intentional. Who can you bless today by expressing your gratitude? Think of someone and pick up the phone to call them, send them a gratitude text, put a card in the mail or treat them to something nice. Each day we can find ways to express our gratitude. Let's wake up and go to bed with an attitude of gratitude!

Chapter Eight

THE *H* PRINCIPLES

Home

I HAVE THIS PICTURE IN MY HOUSE THAT SAYS, "HOME IS WHERE YOUR STORY begins!" Think about it. Many of our parents gave birth to us in the hospital and brought us home. Most likely, we did the same thing. The first place that we were taken after leaving the hospital was home. No matter how big or how small, you were brought home. Home is where our stories began. It really is the first place where we start to learn.

We learn how to love, talk, walk, sit at a table, eat food and drink, wash our face, brush our teeth, get dressed, say our prayers, use our manners, do our chores and the list goes on and on. There are so many things that we learn in the home. We learn good things and sometimes we learn bad things. Our first teachers are usually our parents. Parents are homeschooling whether they call it homeschooling or not. Children learn just by observing their parents on a day to day basis in the home.

Homeschooling takes place all throughout the home. However, when you decide to be intentional about homeschooling, you should select a dedicated place where school will take place. If you have a spare room or area that you can use, transform it into a classroom. Decorate the room and allow your children to help. We had a classroom in the basement of our home and this worked out well for the first few years of homeschooling. Once my daughter started high school, she was allowed to work in her bedroom at her desk or wherever she felt most comfortable. If you do not have an extra room or area, use what you have. Oftentimes families use the kitchen and set their students up at the kitchen table. When the kitchen table is used, families have to be flexible. They eat their meals at the table, then clear the table to place their books on the table for school. When space is an issue, you make the best out of what you have.

One of the challenges that I have heard some homeschool moms discuss is that it is difficult to keep the home neat and clean while homeschooling multiple children. When you have papers, crayons, books, and all kinds of learning tools all over the place, it is challenging and I really understand. However, the key is staying organized, assigning chores and having a consistent clean up time after school is over. Not keeping the house tidy can create issues for your husband and for everyone else. Remember your children are learning just by watching how you keep your house. Children have to be taught how to maintain the house. After they are taught, they must be held accountable for their chores and the things that need to be done to maintain a neat and clean house.

High School

WHEN I FIRST BEGAN HOMESCHOOLING, it was not my desire to homeschool through high school. I was scared of the thought of teaching high school science and math. At the time, I didn't know about any other options. Since my son went back to a traditional school in the 6th grade, I only had to focus on homeschooling my daughter. When my daughter finished the middle school years, we thought about where she would attend high school. As my husband and I discussed Ciara's homeschooling journey, we recognized that she was doing well and that homeschooling was working for her. Therefore, we decided to continue homeschooling her throughout high school. One of the things that encouraged me to continue was finding out that I did not have to personally teach all of her high school courses, I could pay for her to take the classes that I could not teach. I was so happy to know that Ciara could get her math, science and other courses from a facility that was specifically for homeschoolers and also at the community college. Between the two, my daughter was able to get everything that she needed.

One of the common questions that people ask about homeschooling through high school is what about graduation and will my child be able to experience having a prom? Since we signed up to be a part of a homeschooling umbrella, my daughter was able to participate in a beautiful graduation ceremony and attend a prom that was especially for homeschoolers in the Maryland area. As parents of a high school student, you are the one who helps your child create memorable experiences. Get them involved and connected with opportunities and events that will help to develop and enrich your child's high school years.

One question that my daughter had when we decided to homeschool through high school was; "Will I be able to go on a class trip?" These are things that she had heard that other high schoolers were doing and she wanted to know if she would be able to do the same. As a graduation gift, my husband made plans for Ciara to get her wish. She had a class trip to the Bahamas. She and I traveled together to celebrate the completion of high school.

I believe that my daughter thought that since she did not attend a traditional high school, she had missed out on something. I had to reassure her that she wasn't missing anything. My daughter was able to enjoy her high school years because of the various activities, trips and opportunities that were provided. As I mentioned, she completed most of her high school requirements in the 11th grade and started taking courses at the community college during her senior year.

Homeschooling

IS HOMESCHOOLING FULL TIME THE BEST THING FOR EVERY CHILD? Maybe not but every child can learn something at home. This is not a new thing. Parents have been teaching their children at home since the beginning of time. However, based on history, the official start of actually using the term "homeschooling" goes back to the 1970s. As I researched the topic, I learned that a man by the name of John Holt started the homeschooling movement because he did not like what children were learning from their formal education. He suggested that parents start "unschooling" their children. Many were inspired to homeschool. As the years progress, more and more families are choosing to homeschool for various reasons. Homeschooling is not easy but it is less challenging because of all the different resources that are available today. Having the use of the internet, the ability to take online courses, and taking courses at a community college or other educational facility are options that were not available in the early years of homeschooling.

Homeschooling is a legal alternative to sending your child to a public or private school. It is when parents take the responsibility of educating their children. Parents actually teach their children or hire a tutor or teacher to assist in educating their child. They purchase everything that is needed to help educate their children. Homeschooling is normally done at home but it can take place at other places such as church, library, museums, etc. One of the great things about homeschooling is that you can select the courses that you want your child to have. Yes, there are some standard things that have to be taught based on the state that you live in. However, you can expose your child to whatever you would like. Think about it. It's like going to a restaurant and looking at the menu to select all of your favorite foods. You can select whatever your taste buds desire. I love the fact that homeschooling allowed me to select courses and activities that I want my children to have, some of which were not being taught in their traditional school, for example, banking and financial literacy.

I believe that it is a privilege to homeschool your children. Due to Covid-19 and social distancing, many children were not able to learn in their school buildings during the 2020 school year. Many schools provided distance learning which allowed children to learn at home through the use of the computer. Distance learning usually means teachers provide the instruction and assignments for students as well as grade and evaluate them from a distance. Parents can help their children and oversee their child's work. Although distance learning is done at home and can allow you to get a taste of what homeschooling is like, it is not the same as homeschooling full time. Distance learning is driven by the school and the teachers assigning the work. Teachers also select the curriculum, teach lessons, and evaluate work. Parents only have to oversee what the teachers have assigned and depending on the age of their child, they may have to help their child complete the work. This created an issue for many parents especially those who work from home. I have heard parents complain because some were doing more school work with their children than ever before and it was very time consuming. Although distance learning can be challenging, the overall instruction is in the hands of the school system.

Some families like distance learning and some do not. Some parents have decided to totally homeschool their children (full time) the next school year as a result of them liking the distance learning experience with their children. On the other hand, there were parents who were frustrated with their children being at home and can't wait for them to go back to the school building to learn. Parents who are homeschooling full time are totally responsible for providing their child's education.

Regardless of the circumstances, if you have the opportunity to homeschool, see it as a privilege and enjoy every moment. You only get one shot at raising your children; do your best. Homeschooling is a sacrifice, but it is worth it! You get to see your child's progress year after year and experience their education with them. I often told myself, "You can always get a job and go back to work but you can't always raise your children and educate them." Our children don't stay school aged forever. The time that you spend homeschooling is priceless!

Help

THERE IS NO WAY THAT I COULD HAVE SUCCESSFULLY HOMESCHOOLED without help. I am so thankful for my help during our seven years' journey of homeschooling. I had help in so many different ways such as: having someone to tutor my daughter and teach her classes that I could not teach, help with transporting my daughter from one place to another, help with making various decisions concerning homeschooling, etc. Once I decided to homeschool, I began meeting and connecting with several homeschooling moms and people who made themselves available to help me. If you are planning to take the homeschooling journey, you will not be alone. There is a large homeschool community out there and you will find the help that you need. Some of the moms were experienced homeschoolers and were a big help just by sharing their experiences. I would always ask questions. If you don't ask for help and ask others to share, you are likely to get overwhelmed with everything required for homeschooling.

It is so important to network and develop a homeschooling support group that will help you on your journey. You don't want to be isolated and lonely on this journey. Homeschooling alone is the opposite route that most people will take so if you do not connect with someone you will feel alone and frustrated. It is important to have other people who are experienced in homeschooling to be a sounding board for your thoughts, ideas, concerns and to provide advice. Whenever I would get together with moms who had been homeschooling for years, we would talk about their experiences, lessons learned, and I was like a sponge trying to soak it all up. I wanted to learn as much as I could. Just like it is important for children to socialize with other children and to not feel alone, it is also important for parents! Homeschooling is not a journey that you should take alone. You will need help!

There is help available. You can get help from other homeschooling families in your community, help online, help from the state that you live in, attend homeschooling conferences and read as many books as you can on homeschooling. As you are making your homeschool plans, give careful thought to your child's education, consider your child, what you should teach, the curriculum, activities and everything. Think about where you will need help and the people who are already in your life who may be able to help you or they may know someone who can help. Having good help makes the homeschooling journey so much easier.

Chapter Nine

THE I PRINCIPLES

Independence

ONE OF THE MOST VALUABLE SKILLS THAT I THINK STUDENTS SHOULD HAVE IS the ability to work independently. To be independent means that students can work alone when they need to; they have an inner drive that pushes them to get the work done with little or no supervision. These students want to learn and they are committed to learning and getting their work done. Independent students can be taught and given a task to complete and they are able to go and complete the task without someone standing over them. They are able to stay focused on the task until completion and you don't have to keep checking on them until the assignment is done. Some students naturally work this way and others have to be taught to work independently. Children are different but when you see a child who can work independently, celebrate this skill.

When a child can work independently, you can teach and map out the assignments for the week and they will work until the assignments are done. This can be very helpful to a mom who has multiple children to homeschool. You can teach your independent student a lesson, give them assignments and begin working with your other homeschoolers. If you are just homeschooling one child who is independent, you will be able to get other things done while your child is working. Their ability to work independently will free you up.

One of the reasons why this is such a valuable skill to have is that it can be carried into college. Students who are successful in college have often mastered the ability to work independently. They go to class a couple times a week, listen to the professor and then have the rest of the week to work independently. Of course, they can pair up with a study partner or a study group, but they are individually responsible for getting the job done. No one is standing over them throughout the week to help them get the job done; they must work independently.

Although the ability to work independently is a blessing, it can be taken the wrong way if there is no balance. When students work independently but don't have the ability to work with others, this is a problem. In college, there are various assignments that require students to work together in pairs or groups. If your student cannot work with others, this will create a problem. So, although independence should be encouraged and celebrated, we must also make sure that our students are able to work well with others.

Information

PEOPLE ARE DESTROYED AND PENALIZED FOR WHAT THEY DON'T KNOW, in other words, a lack of knowledge. There are so many things to learn about homeschooling. If you are thinking about homeschooling or have already made a decision to homeschool, it is very important to gather as much information as possible. Use various resources to get informed. Go online, attend a homeschool conference, talk to experienced homeschooling parents, read books and find out all that you can. The more information that you gather the more informed you can be about homeschooling.

When decisions impact your family and your finances, you definitely need to gather as much information as possible. The decision to homeschool is a major decision and there are a lot of things to consider. The more information you gather up front, the more prepared you can be to have a successful homeschooling experience. As far as homeschooling is concerned, our children can miss out if we are not well informed.

It is very important to be informed on the learning requirements for each school year. As a homeschooling parent you will need to be aware of everything that your child is expected to know so that you can be intentional about what you will teach. You will also need to be informed on the state requirements for homeschoolers. Each state may have differences

in what they require for homeschoolers and for students who will graduate from a high school. Some of the traditional schools require that students complete a certain number of community service hours before graduation; you will need to see if this applies to your homeschooler.

Inner Circle

HAVING A GOOD INNER CIRCLE CAN BE JUST THE FUEL THAT YOU NEED to keep going. A good inner circle will inspire, coach, motivate and encourage you to keep homeschooling on those days where it gets tough. Not everyone will be supportive so if you don't have a good inner circle, you will need to search for it and create it. Establish an inner circle with people who have homeschooled before and people who are currently homeschooling. It is great when you meet people with the same aged children. You can discuss ideas, lesson plans and activities that you are planning. If you know educators or teachers who are willing to share best practices or just encourage you along the way, these may be people to include in your inner circle. Having family and friends who will make themselves available to relieve and support you makes a world of difference. Oftentimes when you are doing something for the first time, your mind is filled with self-doubt and thoughts that can deter you from continuing. When you feel like you can't make it, you need to be able to connect with your inner circle.

Not only is an inner circle of friends important for the homeschooling parent, it is also important for your children. Most likely, your friends will have children who can become friends with your children. It is good for your children to have an inner circle of friends who can be there throughout their homeschooling journey. It also helps when you have friends whose children are a little older and further ahead on the journey so that your children can see the road ahead. It's also good for you to see the success of parents who have been homeschooling for years and some whose children have graduated.

Having experienced moms in my inner circle was truly a blessing. I loved hearing their stories and meeting their children. Some were no longer children but adults who were thriving because of their homeschooling experience. The world may not embrace the idea of homeschooling but if you have an inner circle who will support you, you will be more likely to stay the course. Do some research in your local community and see if there are other homeschooling families. Remember, if you don't have a good inner circle, you can create one.

Image

DO YOU HAVE A MENTAL IMAGE OF WHAT HOMESCHOOLING should look like? Where did you get that image? Homeschooling may look different for each family. How it is done and what it looks like in your home may be different from how it looks in someone else's home. Realize that you have to set up your homeschool based on what works for your family.

Each year that you homeschool may look differently based on the seasons and growth of your family. Be willing to be flexible to get the job done. If you are homeschooling and something happens to a member of your family, you may have to divide yourself so that you are homeschooling your child and caring for the needs of your sick child, spouse or a parent. As challenging as it may be, homeschooling must continue while meeting the needs of family.

One year our homeschooling environment changed because of a flood in our basement. We were accustomed to having school in our classroom which was located in the basement. Being in the classroom helped me to stay focused. When I went into the classroom, it forced me to totally focus on homeschooling. However, when we had a flood in our basement, we had to homeschool upstairs in the kitchen. Being in the kitchen was hard for me because there were other things to do in the kitchen and I was on the same floor of my office. I began trying to multitask while my daughter was doing her work. I began taking phone calls during our homeschooling time. Since we were near the office, I would check the mail and give attention to other things in the office. Being upstairs was more of a distraction for me

The I Principles

and my daughter noticed it. She said, "Daddy, can you hurry up and fix the basement because mommy keeps getting distracted up here." After Ciara made this comment, I had to readjust and focus. Something had happened in our household which changed the dynamics of our homeschool, and I needed to stay focused. Even though we were out of our normal teaching environment, I still needed to be dedicated and focused to get the job done instead of getting distracted by other areas of the home.

It is a good thing for your children to be exposed to positive homeschooling images. Be sure to expose your children to other children who are thriving and who have successfully graduated from the homeschool community. Although homeschooling may look different in each household, having a positive image of homeschooling is important.

Chapter Ten
THE J PRINCIPLES

Job

HOMESCHOOLING IS A FULL-TIME JOB! HOWEVER, THERE ARE PARENTS WHO homeschool during the day and work another job at night. I have met a couple of moms who were nurses that worked the night shift in order to homeschool their children during the day. Once you decide to homeschool your child, it is a good thing to see homeschooling as your job. It is a job that you are responsible for each day especially Monday through Friday when school is in session.

When you see homeschooling as a job, you will get up, get dressed and be prepared just as you would for any other job. You will also need to allocate a certain amount of time for your job and schedule in a lunch. When you are at work and you have done your time, you leave to go home. The difference with homeschooling is that you are already home. Therefore, when you are done with homeschooling you must transition and close school for the day. School ends, and all of your other responsibilities kick in like dinner and preparing for your spouse to come home or whatever you have going on in the evening. Although when you homeschool, your children are always learning even when school is out. There are things that children learn such as how to maintain the house, chores, cooking, ironing and the list goes on and on.

If parents and students do not think of homeschooling as a job that they must be committed to, there will be problems. They are more likely not to have enough work completed by the end of the school year. Families must be committed and have the discipline to put in a full day's work on a consistent basis realizing that they have been called to do this job and to do it well.

Joy

IN SPITE OF ALL THE CHALLENGES AND MY INSECURITIES with being able to successfully homeschool, I must say that overall, it was a joy! By joy I mean it really brought happiness to me to see my children learning firsthand. There are some lessons I wanted to teach my children and I didn't want to hear about them from someone else. It was so satisfying to know that my daughter was equipped with everything that she needed to make it to college and then to graduate with honors. As parents, we have been given the responsibility to train our children and when you have spent time teaching them something, it brings joy to see them sharing or doing something that you taught them. Homeschooling provides you with the opportunity to be intentional about teaching everything that you want your children to learn. What a joy!

Having the privilege of homeschooling is something to be joyful about. Some people wish that they could but for whatever the reason, they are not able. I know it sometimes seems like you will be raising and training your children forever, but this is not the case. Remind yourself that your children will only be school aged for a season. Choosing to have joy brings longevity to the journey. If you dread having to homeschool your children, you will make the journey more challenging and may not make it. Having joy in the midst of teaching and raising your children gives you strength each day to maintain consistency. There will be some days where you may not feel like homeschooling, but when you reflect on the joy and privilege that you have it gives you strength to keep going.

Your attitude will definitely impact your children's homeschooling experience. Joy is contagious. If you have a joyful heart in homeschooling your children, your children will be able to feel the joy. Your perspective makes a world of difference so count it all joy!

The J Principles

Joining Each Other

ONE OF THE THINGS THAT MADE HOMESCHOOLING PLEASANT for me and my children was being able to join other homeschooling families. When I was homeschooling my son and my daughter, there were some lessons that I could teach to both of them. The two of them would join for some lessons and it made it a lot more interesting. What was more interesting was when we were able to join another family or other homeschooling students.

While being a part of the homeschool umbrella, my daughter met another young lady around her age. She needed to take the same history course as my daughter, so I was able to teach the two of them together. I gave them assignments to work on throughout the week, but we would physically join each other at the library once a week for the class. We reserved a room and were consistent with reading, discussing and conducting class. Joining each other at a different location made history more interesting for both girls.

On another occasion, one mom decided to have an art class at her house. She invited a few homeschooling moms and their children to attend. She had someone to come and share about art and our children painted pictures. They had a lesson, created a piece of art and had lunch together. It was so nice for our children to learn and experience art together.

During my daughter's senior year, we joined other groups for several events. There was a homeschooling prom for all the homeschoolers in the area. Many of the homeschoolers who were seniors wanted to experience going to a prom. Therefore, a group of moms and graduates joined to plan the event and it was very nice. A nice venue was selected and the graduates got dressed up to attend. We also joined with the other graduates under the homeschooling umbrella to take senior portraits. A photographer was hired and several of us scheduled a time for our seniors to take their pictures. This was great because we didn't have to make our own arrangements for the pictures. Lastly, because we were under the homeschooling umbrella, we joined each other for the graduation. There was a lovely homeschool graduation with caps, gowns and tassels. The graduating group was small, so it was very personalized with pictures of each graduate and a write up about each of their homeschooling journeys. The homeschooling director along with parents were able to stand behind their graduates and pray with each of them as they closed out their senior year and launched into the next part of their journey. Joining with other homeschooling families made this event more enjoyable and memorable.

Juggle

HOMESCHOOLING DEFINITELY REQUIRES PARENTS TO JUGGLE! When I first started homeschooling, I did not work outside of the home. After I had some years under my belt, I began working under a homeschool umbrella. I taught a few homeschool courses and later became a homeschool evaluator. Both jobs were conducive to homeschooling. As a teacher, I was able to teach classes in the same building that my daughter was taking classes. Being a homeschool evaluator required me to meet with other homeschooling families. I enjoyed meeting with other parents and homeschooling students because it was nice to help other families on their journey.

In addition to working part-time, I was juggling other things such as: housework, grocery shopping, ministry work, various activities and time with my husband. For three years I juggled homeschooling my son and my daughter together. When my son returned to the traditional school setting, I still had to juggle. I juggled helping him with his assignments, attending his events while still homeschooling my daughter. I had to make sure that my daughter was getting everything she needed for high school and to prepare for college. As parents with school-aged children, the need to juggle continues.

In order to successfully juggle everything, it is wise to keep a calendar of all of your and your children's events and activities. Also, make a "things to do" list so that you can remember everything that needs to be done. This will help you to stay organized. If you are juggling too much, you may have to take something off your plate and just focus on what has to be done each day. Juggling is a great skill to have but not everyone can juggle well!

Chapter Eleven
THE K PRINCIPLES

Keeper

ARE YOU A KEEPER OF THE HOME? WHEN I THINK OF THE KEEPER OF THE HOME, I think of one who keeps the house clean and maintains order. However, being the keeper of the home can mean so much more. If you have decided to homeschool, it is very likely that most of your child's education will take place in the home. The home can be a great place to educate your children or it can be a place where more harm than good is done. If you understand the role of a keeper, your home can be safe and healthy for everyone.

Being a stay at home wife and mother full time made it easier for me to be a keeper of the home. One of the keys to being a good keeper is to spend more time in your home. The truth of the matter is that you can't be a good keeper if you are never home. A keeper is a person who guards or watches over something. Parents have been given the responsibility to watch over and protect their children. If the wife is the parent who is home the most (in some cases it is the husband), then she will be the best parent to be the keeper of the home. This means that she maintains the home and watches everything going and coming into the home. Some things are just not appropriate to be brought into the home. A good keeper is aware of what is coming and going out of their home.

As a homeschooling parent, you are the keeper of your child's education. Although there are basic requirements that each state has, you are responsible for what your child will learn. You get to decide the additional subjects that you want your child to learn. You can also decide the way in which your child will learn. Part of being a good homeschooling keeper is making sure that your child gets everything that they need to learn. You provide a good learning environment, curriculum, consistency and lots of love. You are your child's number one teacher. Yes, they will have classes that they take from other sources, but you are primarily responsible for the overall education of your child. Be a good keeper!

Kindergarten

ONE OF THE GOALS OF KINDERGARTEN IS TO PROVIDE CURRICULUM, skills and rich activities that will encourage children to want to learn more. Although both of my children went to a traditional school for kindergarten, I started homeschooling before they went to school. I admire the parents who made a decision to homeschool their children before they were born. Some made the plan to homeschool in advance; therefore, their children have never experienced a traditional school environment.

Kindergarten is where most traditional schools start; however, we know that our children are learning way before kindergarten. Parents who begin educating their children before kindergarten provide a much stronger start for their children. When my children were under the age of five, I didn't realize that I was homeschooling them then. I bought educational toys, books and charts with visuals to begin teaching them. There are some things that children will naturally learn from the day-to-day routines of life. Children observe everything that we do, the good and the bad. Someone once said, "They will learn what is taught and some things are just caught."

Since Kindergarten marks the traditional beginning of school, each child deserves a strong start. Parents can help their child to start strong by homeschooling. I remember teaching my children their ABC's, 123's and how to identify common things like animals, fruits and certain foods. Monday through Friday we would have some form of school time. The public library and some of the private book stores offer story time for toddlers. Each week I would take my children to either the bookstore or the library to listen to a story with other children. After story time, I would allow them to select a book to take home. The thing that I loved about the library is that the books were free! When we went to the bookstore for story time, I would often end up spending money to purchase a book. It's funny because my son took a liking to reading brand new books over the library books. I think this is because he would sometimes come across library books that had marks or stains from someone else's use. My goal was to get them familiar with the whole idea of listening to books being read, reading small words and turning the pages of the books. They were also familiar with sitting still and being quiet while reading was taking place.

In a traditional school, many kindergarten programs test children before they begin. Schools want to determine which level of kindergarten is best for them. I used to think kindergarten was all the same, but I later learned that there are different levels. In one class they may have to start from scratch with their ABC's and 123's and in another class, the kids already know these things so they can move on to learning other things. If your child has not been homeschooled or had some prior form of school before they go to kindergarten, it is unlikely that they will test well. Some parents are okay with that; however, my desire was to give my kids the best start possible. I homeschooled before they went to kindergarten not knowing that I would later choose to homeschool on a full-time basis. Homeschooling before kindergarten is key to giving your child a strong start!

Kids

IT DOESN'T MATTER IF YOU REFER TO THEM AS KIDS OR AS CHILDREN, they are all precious gifts from God. It is truly an honor to be able to give birth or even to adopt. Some have inherited other people's children because of various situations with their family and friends. No matter what the situation, when God places a human being in your hands to raise, He holds you responsible for how you love, nurture and take care of them. You really only have one chance to raise your children and the time goes by so fast.

We must seek the Lord on behalf of the gifts that have been placed in our care. My prayer has been, "Lord teach me how to raise these precious gifts that you have given me." I know that God loves them more than I could ever love them, so I rely on Him to lead me and guide me. I have asked the Lord to show me the plans and the thoughts that He thinks towards them so that I can help encourage them and lead them in the right path.

One of our most important responsibilities concerning our kids is to teach them about God. Raising kids is one thing but can you raise a godly seed? We must live our lives in such a way that our children learn about God and it is our job to teach them how to have a relationship with God. The Bible says train them up in the way that they should go and when they are old they will not depart from it. (Proverbs 22:6). We must train them to go to church, worship God, say their prayers and to make room for God in their day-to-day life. Children learn so much by the way that we live our lives. Now we know that none of us is perfect, so the only perfect role model is Christ. However, if we stay close to Christ on the journey of being a parent, we should be able to provide a decent example and be decent role models for our kids to see.

Praying for your kids gives you insight from God. Each of our children is different and therefore, they have different needs. Some of their needs are met best when we as parents step in to help. Making sure that our children are educated is another one of our responsibilities as a parent. There are so many choices: public school, private school and homeschool. Homeschooling is an avenue that allows parents to step in and provide an education that is especially tailored for the gift that God has given you.

Kitchen

SO MANY LESSONS ARE TAUGHT AND LEARNED IN THE KITCHEN. This is truly a family gathering place. Meals are prepared and eaten at the table while the same table is often used for homeschooling. For those who may not have a designated homeschooling classroom, the kitchen serves the purpose. In most cases, there is a table with chairs and this is where it all begins. Sitting at the table, pulling out curriculum and teaching valuable lessons is an everyday routine for many who homeschool. When you don't have the space for a designated classroom in the home, you use what you have. The kitchen works!

The K Principles

When you are homeschooling young children, there are so many lessons that can be taught in the kitchen. I remember when my children were younger and before I officially started homeschooling, I would teach lessons in the kitchen. I found this flip chart that had colored pictures of the ABC's, fruits, shapes and other common pictures to identify. During the week, I would sit in the kitchen with my son and daughter before they went to kindergarten and review the pictures and letters on the chart. It was a part of our daily routine until they could identify everything on the chart. We sat in the kitchen at the table for many lessons.

The kitchen is also a good place to teach math and cooking skills. Math can be taught as you measure various foods and prepare recipes. You can also count various food items in the kitchen. My children enjoyed our time in the kitchen. We would select various recipes to make and take pictures of the final product. When children are young, you can use the kitchen to help them learn to identify various things like fruits, vegetables, dishes, eating utensils and you can also teach table setting and cleaning skills. It is important for students to learn how to properly clean a kitchen after a meal has been prepared. Cleaning the kitchen after each meal becomes even more crucial when you are using your kitchen to homeschool.

Two things that I was able to teach my children in the kitchen that I didn't learn until I was an adult are 1) How to check for the expiration dates on food items and 2) How to read the food labels and nutrition facts that are usually on the back labels. Once I taught my children about the expiration dates, they learned to check the dates before using things that may have been in the pantry or refrigerator too long. Learning to read the nutrition facts has taught my children to be informed about what they are eating before they eat.

Another lesson that I remember teaching my children in the kitchen is how to say a blessing over their food. They learned to thank God for their food and to bless the meal. This is a discipline that will be practiced for many years. The kitchen is probably one of the most used rooms of the house.

Chapter Twelve
THE L PRINCIPLES

Love

I AM REMINDED OF A PASSAGE THAT SAYS, "LOVE SUFFERS LONG AND IS KIND" (I Corinthians 13:4-7). Homeschooling is an act of sacrificial love. You have to be willing to sacrifice a lot of time and effort to homeschool. It's one thing to send your child to school and help them with the homework that the teacher has assigned. So much more is required when you are the primary teacher and your child is depending on you for their education. Although love is a special ingredient that every good parent has when raising their children, there has to be another level of love in order to homeschool. Parents who decide to homeschool have to have a vision of what they want for their children's education and know how to give it to them.

Since homeschooling requires more from the parents than a traditional school, you have to have a lot of love to start and finish successfully. The love that a parent has for their child's best interests is the love that is necessary for homeschooling. As a parent, you are your child's first teacher and if you start homeschooling from the beginning you will be able to see your child's strengths and weaknesses and how it affects them academically. You will see areas that may be challenging for your child as well as areas that seem to be naturally easy. Having love and patience is what is needed when you see that your child needs to improve in an area or is not working on grade level. Another teacher may get frustrated and give up on working with your child.

However, because of your love and a personal interest in your child, you may get frustrated, but you will keep working with your child to help them succeed. When you can't get the job done, you will find a tutor or outsource a class to help your child. Love doesn't quit!

Love is powerful and it will help to carry you throughout your homeschooling journey. When you get tired and weary, just go to the Ultimate source of Love (Jesus Christ) to get love and keep giving it to your child as you homeschool.

Learning Styles

Many years ago, when I took some education courses, I remember learning that there are seven different types of learning styles. Once you find out your child's learning style, you can be intentional about tailoring your curriculum and teaching to best meet the needs of your child. Every child is different, so it is important to find the method that works best for your child.

The seven learning styles are:

1. **Visual (Spacial):** Learns best by seeing images and visuals.
2. **Auditory (Musical):** Learns well with sound. Most musicians are auditory learners.
3. **Verbal:** Learns best with verbal instruction and writing.
4. **Physical (Kinesthetic):** Learns by using their hands or physically doing something.
5. **Logical:** Learns in a unique way. Mathematically inclined and thinks logically.
6. **Social:** Likes to learn with other students. They love group work and extracurricular activities.
7. **Solitary:** Does not have to be around a group of other students. Prefers to learn on their own.

Knowing your child's learning style could very well be the key to successfully educating your child. Learn your child's style and be intentional about using their style for everything.

Legal

IS HOMESCHOOLING LEGAL? Yes! It is legal but that has not always been the case. In the early 1980's, homeschooling was not legal in most states. Today homeschooling is legal in all 50 of the United States. If you are planning to homeschool, you should check with the state to learn their specific educational law requirements. Some states are more strict than others and have strict requirements. Therefore, it is important that you are aware of what is expected of you and your child.

I homeschooled my children in the state of Maryland. Some of the things that I was required to do by law were: 1) Notify the state that I was withdrawing my children from the traditional school setting. 2) Teach the subjects that were required for each grade level.

3) Commit to giving my children the required instruction needed. 4) Maintain a portfolio of all my children's work. 5) Respond to any request that may have come from the state.

When your child turns 5 years old, parents are legally responsible for their child's education and should take it seriously. Providing a structured homeschool environment usually provides the best learning experiences. Although parents can run their homeschool any way they would like, I made every effort to provide a more structured environment for my children. By structure, I mean we were intentional about having a daily schedule and following it for the most part. Of course, we had some days where we didn't go by the schedule. However, on most days, we got up, got dressed and started school at the same time each day. Each of my children were given a specific amount of time in each subject and if more time was needed, they were given more time. I graded their work, gave feedback and recorded their grades in a gradebook. All of their papers were stored in their portfolio. On most days, they worked in a room dedicated to their classroom with a desk, chair and a whiteboard. Having structure made everything easier when it was time to be evaluated.

When it comes to legal matters, it is a good idea to be a member of HSLDA, the Home School Legal Defense Association. It is a non-profit organization that helps to protect homeschooling families in the event you have any legal issues. There is a small fee to join and homeschooling families are provided with: peace of mind, experienced legal help, advice, encouragement and support for the homeschooling journey. HSLDA helps to equip families for successful homeschooling. They will help with questions and decisions that will need to be made.

Library

THE PUBLIC LIBRARY IS A GREAT RESOURCE FOR HOMESCHOOLING. In fact, it is a great resource even if you are not homeschooling. I found it very beneficial to introduce my children to the library at an early age. Each of them had their own library card and became accustomed to checking out their own materials. The library is filled with books, periodicals and videos that are very helpful in educating your children. Some subjects were introduced by finding a library book on the subject. We also checked out videos that helped to explain something that we were learning.

Going to the library was one of the trips that I enjoyed. We started our trips to the library when my kids were preschoolers. As parents of preschoolers, we took advantage of the free story-time offered by the Librarian. This became a weekly field trip in our household. My children enjoyed going to the library, picking out books and checking them out. They would read them in the car and take them home to practice reading throughout the week.

As my children got older, we used the library as a study hall. I taught history to my daughter and another homeschooler in the library. We would reserve a room in the library and meet every week to read, learn, study and discuss history. This was one way of making history interesting to two teenage girls. Sometimes we would meet to take a history-related field trip instead of staying at the library.

During my daughter's junior year, we went to the library and collected information on the state scholarships that were available. Our local library had great resources for students preparing for college. It is important that your children learn the art of finding information. I know that we now have the use of the internet and therefore, students have everything they need at their fingertips. However, knowing how to read and conduct research is a valuable skill. If you introduce your children to the library in their early years, it will enhance their reading and research skills.

Chapter Thirteen

THE *M* PRINCIPLES

Manage

AS A HOMESCHOOLING PARENT YOU NEED TO BE A GOOD MANAGER! YOU ARE responsible for doing something that most people put into the hands of someone else: their child's education. Managing is such a vital skill because as a homeschooling parent you often have to allocate time to homeschool, take care of yourself, your family, your home and any other responsibilities that you may have. Homeschooling is very time consuming so the better you learn to manage your time, the more you can get done on any given day.

As a good manager, it is important to start with a schedule. Write out all of the subjects and activities for the week and decide how much time you will spend on each. Planning is the key. You should have a plan for the school year with the curriculum that needs to be taught, a weekly/daily plan that will allow your homeschooler time to get the work done. Managing time adequately each day is very important. The days will go by quickly and before you know it, a quarter is gone and you will be expected to provide evidence of your homeschooling to a homeschool reviewer. The way that you manage your time will determine your success.

Each day that I was homeschooling, I had to really discipline myself to manage my time. There were days when my housework, ministry work and other things came up during my homeschooling time. I had to resist the temptation to do other things when it was my homeschooling time. There were some days when I was able to multitask but for most days, I totally dedicated my time to homeschooling during the school hours. When you don't manage your time well, you will lose time and not be as productive.

Another thing that needs to be well-managed when you are homeschooling is keeping up with the necessary requirements for your particular state. You have to make sure that you will have work samples, a portfolio and whatever else you need to satisfy the state requirements. If you are a good manager, your homeschooling reviews will go well.

Memories

HOMESCHOOLING WILL COME TO AN END, but the memories will last forever! One of the many benefits of homeschooling is being able to create the types of educational memories that you want your child to have. Hopefully, you will create good memories of you spending time investing in your child and creating activities to help enrich their educational journey. Children will always remember the love and the time that was spent with them. In order to create good memories for your child, you should start homeschooling with the end in mind. What is it that you want your children to say about their homeschooling experience? What type of character, skills and experiences would you like for them to gain from their homeschool journey? When you think about the answers to these questions, you will need to create experiences that will cultivate the type of outcome that you would like to have.

As you schedule and plan your child's lessons each week, you should think of things to do that would help your child to learn something as well as create a good memory. For example, if you are teaching history, you may teach the lesson and then plan a trip to a museum that provides more information on that area of time. If you are teaching a geography lesson and one of the places your child is interested in is New York City, plan a trip. Go to New York and create a memory so that your child can actually experience New York. There is nothing like being able to go and see a place that you have read about in a book. You will create memories each time that you go and experience a different place.

Always remember to take pictures to capture each memory. Pictures help to tell the story and can be used in your child's homeschooling portfolio.

The great thing is that your children will always be able to look back on what they did while on their homeschooling journey.

Movies

AS A HOMESCHOOLING PARENT, it is good to switch things up from time to time. There are so many ways that children can learn; you don't have to do things the same way every day. There were some days that we incorporated a movie into our homeschooling schedule. You can find a movie on just about any topic and tie it in to lessons you want your children to learn. There were days when I found a movie from the library that we would check out and watch. At other times, we would actually go out for a movie at a theater. After the movie, I would always ask, "What did you learn from the movie?" If you want to really make it into an assignment and depending upon the age of your homeschooler, you could have your children write a paragraph or a short essay to summarize the movie and to share any lessons learned.

Another way to make going to the movie theater an educational experience (again it depends on the age of your homeschooler), you could have students purchase tickets online. Check out the price of the movie and have them compare the cost to another movie theater. They could also do a little research on the movie they are going to see. Who are the actors and actresses? Have them find out if the movie is fiction or nonfiction. How many stars does the movie have and what are the critics saying? All these things are lessons that homeschoolers can learn around watching or going to a movie theater. There are so many things that students can learn from a movie.

Music

MUSIC IS A GREAT EDUCATIONAL TOOL! Studies reveal that songs, lyrics and other musical elements can be used as a method of teaching and learning. One of the first educational songs that many of us learned was the ABC song. We sang this song over and over until we learned our alphabets. I am a firm believer in using music to promote learning and to improve academic performance of students.

In addition to the ABC song, there are various lessons that my children have learned by way of music. They have learned the books of the Bible and various Bible verses in a song. Both were songs that I totally made up. When my daughter was in private school, she learned the names of the United States Presidents by singing, "The President's Song." When it was time to learn the multiplication table, my children also learned it in a song. The great thing about a song is that they can listen to it or sing it over and over again. Repetition helps with memorization.

Now some families are more musically inclined than others. What I mean by that is they have great singers and instrument players in their family. That is not the case for me, but I love to listen to music and use music as a tool. I also tried to incorporate learning something about music in our homeschooling curriculum. I taught various lessons on instruments and the different kinds of instruments. I even signed my children up for a music class under Maryland Park and Planning. We bought a keyboard and the kids had fun trying to learn how to play the instrument. We planned a music field trip and went to the Kennedy Center one evening to hear various instruments played.

There were several homeschooling mornings that we played upbeat music to help us get started. We would do a few minutes of exercise to a song to get our blood circulating and to have some energy for school. As a teacher, I have also played soft instrumental music in the background while my students were working on various assignments. It seems to relax them. Whenever you want to give students a specific amount of time to do something, you can use a timer with music for children and make it fun. There are a variety of online timers that have music. For example, there is one called Mr. Timer; it provides a 10-minute countdown. In my experience, children love to listen to the music timer; it lets them know that they have a designated amount of time to work on a certain assignment.

Music can set the mood for whatever you want to accomplish and it can also be a great tool to help your children learn. Incorporate music as often as you can.

Chapter Fourteen
THE N PRINCIPLES

Neatly

Homeschooling and working neatly may not happen naturally, but it's actually a great combination. I believe some people are naturally neat and others have to work a little harder. I would be in the second category. It doesn't come naturally for me. I have to be intentional and work at it on a regular basis. I think some areas are easier than others, but I want to encourage homeschooling families to be intentional about doing things neatly. When you are neat, it will pay off. Let me explain what I mean.

When things are done neatly, they are done in a pleasingly orderly way. Everything is in a clean condition and rooms are left with everything in place. It means developing the habit of being orderly and keeping things orderly on a daily basis. Now we know that there will be some days where things may get out of order, but this would be an exception and not the norm. When the house or the rooms are neat, they are clean and pleasing in appearance. Being neat is beneficial whether you are homeschooling or not. It is particularly important that homeschooling parents not only practice doing things neatly but encourage their children to do the same.

Doing things neatly is a skill and it should be taught as you are raising your children. Now if you don't naturally have the skill (like me), you will have to work at it and keep practicing it. Children will follow your lead and watch what you do. One of my goals was and still is to maintain neatness in our home, especially in the areas that we work in the most like in our classroom and in the kitchen. I also had to teach my children how to make their rooms neat; even though they may not always put this into practice, they know how.

As it relates to school, children should be taught how to do their work neatly. Teach them to take pride in how they write their name, how they turn in their work and remind them that their work is a reflection of them. Homeschooling parents should keep a neat collection of their children's work so that they can proudly display what their children have been doing on a weekly basis. Doing things neatly will pay off!

Negativity

WHEN YOU DECIDE THAT YOU ARE GOING TO HOMESCHOOL or are even thinking about the possibility, please don't expect everyone to give you a positive response. I received so much negativity from people when I mentioned homeschooling. Some were solicited comments and many were unsolicited.

One of the most common concerns that people have is socialization. How will homeschooled children interact with others? Will they be able to conduct themselves around others? People who don't know any better assume that homeschooled children will have problems with socialization. Although this is not the case for many homeschoolers, they picture parents being in the house with their children from day to day with no interaction with others. Therefore, they tend to make negative comments about children who are homeschooled.

Some of the negativity comes from children who are in traditional schools. They make fun of or tease children who are homeschooled. Some of the negative comments include: 1) There must be something wrong with you since you are not in a regular school. 2) It must be boring spending all day with your mother. 3) You can't possibly be learning something at home all day. 4) Are you really learning? 5) What do you do all day at home? Kids can be really cruel to one another. Not only children but adults too. We cannot allow people to deter us from doing what God has called us to do. Just like with anything else, when God gives you an assignment, you need to do it regardless of the negativity that may come with it. Stay focused!

News

THE WASHINGTON POST NEWSPAPER HAD A SLOGAN that says, "If you don't get it, you don't get it!" I know that the news can be negative but some parts are informative in a good way. One of the things that can help to drive your homeschooling curriculum each week is the "News." What I mean by the news is newly received or noteworthy information, especially about recent or important events. It's a good thing to keep your homeschoolers aware and informed about things that are currently happening in the world. Depending upon the age of your homeschoolers, you can choose age appropriate activities, field trips and assignments to keep them informed.

We were homeschooling during an election year so we listened to the news in reference to the candidates and discussed it in our history class. When President Obama's inauguration took place, we went down on the National Mall to be a part of this historical event. It was an extremely cold day, but we bundled up to be a part of history. Whenever we would take a field trip, I would always assign a writing assignment for my children to express their thoughts, feelings, observations and lessons learned from the trip. We would also take a picture to commemorate the trip. Some days I would give an assignment to listen to the news and give questions to answer about the current event.

Watching the news on television or online was a good way to stay connected with what is happening in the world. In the beginning of our homeschooling days, we used to get the Washington Post newspaper. There are so many educational things that can be done with the newspaper. When my daughter was small and learning how to cut, we would go to the coupon section of the paper, pick out the coupons that we needed and she would practice cutting on the lines. This was a great skill that stayed with my daughter. Now that she is a young adult, she still looks for the best price on things and finds coupons online.

One of the museums that is unfortunately no longer open, specialized in memorable news. It was called the Newseum and was located in Washington, D.C. We made this one of our field trips to experience the various stories and events that had been collected to share in the museum.

The museum was filled with interactive activities and was a great place for homeschoolers to learn. I encourage all homeschooling parents to be intentional about incorporating the day to day news and to find places that you can visit that will help to accomplish this goal.

Oftentimes, people don't like to watch the news because there are a lot of bad things going on and negativity. However, the news helps us to be informed and makes us aware of current events. As the parent, you can be selective about what you want your children to see. Be prepared to have discussions and create assignments around the news. Stay in the know with the news!

No

NO! PRACTICE SAYING IT ONE MORE TIME, "NO." One of the things that I had to do as a homeschooling mom is to learn how to say the word, "NO." You have to practice saying NO to people, places and things that would distract or deter you from having your homeschooling time. Sometimes I had to tell myself, "NO!" NO to talking on the phone during homeschooling time unless it was something urgent. NO to doing other things during the time that I was supposed to be homeschooling. This was a challenge at times because it's something about when people know that you are home during the day. Various opportunities will present themselves to you during the day but you will need to decide if it is something that you need to rearrange your homeschooling schedule for or do you simply need to say, "NO"?

It is so important to let your family and close friends know that although you may be home, you are not available during the school time, whatever your designated time for school. You need to set a standard and stick with it. Everyone should know that while school is in session you are not available. If you were working at a school, or anywhere else, anyone who wanted to reach you would have to wait until you get off work. Therefore, you need to take on the same mindset of being at work because you are at work.

Saying, "NO" is important because when you decide to homeschool, your children's education becomes your number one priority during the week. Your children are counting on you to show up and to be available to give them what they need. If you don't learn to say NO, you and your children will have to deal with the consequences of getting off schedule, being behind and not having enough work completed.

Remember there is a time and a season for everything. Your homeschooling years will only last for a season. You've got to give it all that you have and give your children everything they need to succeed in homeschooling. Practice saying NO!

Chapter Fifteen
THE O PRINCIPLES

One On One

IN A TRADITIONAL CLASSROOM ENVIRONMENT, A TEACHER HAS TO SHARE HIS OR herself with so many children and are rarely able to provide one on one time. One of the many benefits of homeschooling is being available to provide one on one education to your child. You will certainly get to know your child better. You are better able to see your child's strengths and weaknesses some of which you would not know about if you were sending them to a traditional school. As you notice different things about your child, you can tailor your curriculum, activities and your teaching specifically to your child's needs. Another benefit is that you are not forced to stick with something that does not work for your child. When you determine your child's learning style, you should select a curriculum that compliments their learning style. You have the privilege of making changes based on what you want your child to learn and how your child learns.

It is important to remember that God created your child with gifts and talents that need to be discovered and developed. Your homeschooler may have a passion for a particular subject and when you spend one on one time together, you will discover it. As God reveals your child's passions and interests, you can be intentional about having conversations that will stimulate and encourage your child. Also, you can assign meaningful work that will help to develop your child's interest.

If you are homeschooling multiple children, you may be able to teach some subjects together but also be sure to have one on one time with each child. Children love when they can have your undivided attention. You may have to set up a schedule and put your children on a rotation so that each one can have one on one time. This is very important to your child's success.

Options

OPTIONS, OPTIONS, OPTIONS! There are so many different options in homeschooling. You can homeschool under the state or you can homeschool under a homeschooling umbrella. There are a variety of options for curriculum. You can choose traditional books or you can choose online materials. You can teach your child at home in a traditional homeschooling environment or your child can take an online homeschooling class. There are classes that your child can attend under a homeschooling umbrella and depending upon the age of your child, they can take courses at the local community college. There are various extracurricular activities that you can get your child involved in as a homeschooler.

Each day you will be faced with the option of staying in bed and wasting precious homeschooling time or getting up and making every day count. You have to remember that you are on a mission to educate your child and every day is important to the journey. You are responsible for making it happen. If you don't choose the right options, there will be consequences.

You will need to pray about your options and decide what is best for you and your child. Ask God about the decisions that need to be made. Talk to other homeschooling parents and gather information to help you make a wise decision. I remember being a little overwhelmed by all the various decisions that we had to make on the homeschooling journey. Each time God would see us through. He would allow me to connect with someone who was more experienced with homeschooling or present information that would help me with my decision.

Homeschooling is not an option for some people. They can't fathom teaching their own children or may not have the resources to homeschool. It is a blessing to be able to homeschool and choosing the right options has everything to do with you and your child's homeschooling experience. That's why prayer is very important in the process.

Opportunities

HOMESCHOOLING PROVIDES A VARIETY OF OPPORTUNITIES! There were so many things that I was able to accomplish and expose my children to because I was homeschooling. If they were in a traditional school and I was at work outside the home every day, there are many opportunities that we would have missed.

First, we were able to take advantage of trips that required us to be gone during the school day. My children did not have to worry about missing school because we took school wherever they went. Sometimes we took the work with us and other times we scheduled the trip so that we could do the work the next day. One time my son was playing on a football team that made it to the championship. The championship games were held in Florida during the month of December. We were both able to attend the trip and not worry about the time away. Our homeschooling curriculum was easy to carry.

Second, there were activities and things that we were able to participate in during the day. From volunteering to help at the food pantry of the Central Union Mission to helping to make Thanksgiving bags for the needy at our church. We were available and able to take advantage of the opportunities to serve that occurred during the day.

Third, homeschooling allowed me to build closer relationships with my children. I was available to take them places, stay if necessary or pick them up. We were able to find different recipes, prepare meals and eat lunch together. If I was at work all day outside of the home, I definitely would not have the time to select recipes and come home to cook. Teaching children how to prepare meals is a valuable skill. As a result, my daughter was able to go to college and live in an apartment with no campus meal plan. Each week she was able to go grocery shopping and prepare her own meals. This saved us a lot of money and because she is a picky eater, she was able to select and prepare her own meals. What a blessing!

Overwhelming

I HAVE TO ADMIT THAT HOMESCHOOLING CAN BE VERY OVERWHELMING especially when you first get started. I remember feeling the weight of taking on the task of educating my own children and feeling overwhelmed. I knew this was a big responsibility and I was feeling like I didn't know what I was doing. However, I was sure that I had a word from the Lord that homeschooling is what I was supposed to do. In the back of my mind, I also knew that if homeschooling did not work, my children could go back to a traditional school. When I thought about it that way, I said to myself, "We have nothing to lose." I am going to give it my best and take one year at a time. At the end of each year, we will reevaluate to see if we should continue or send them back to a traditional school.

"Now faith is the substance of things hoped for, the evidence of things not seen" (Hebrews 11:1). Homeschooling was truly a journey of faith for me. I started the journey not knowing what it was going to be like but trusting God every step of the way. Each day I would pray and spend time with God for direction concerning my children and our homeschooling journey. God was faithful to give me ideas, lessons and field trips that we would take to enhance my children's learning experience. Also, God would often put people on my heart to call or meet with and they were people who ended up helping me along the way. Being a part of a Homeschooling Umbrella really helped to relieve me of the overwhelming feeling that I had. Knowing that I had access to others who were more experienced than me was a blessing. I think the feeling of being overwhelmed is a common one for new homeschooling parents but as time goes on it gets better and that feeling goes away!

Chapter Sixteen

THE *P* PRINCIPLES

Parents

Did you ever think that you would be a parent and that your children could learn from you? Some things are intentionally taught and others are caught. Think about the lessons that you have learned from your parents without them intentionally teaching you. Many of us have learned so many lessons by simply observing our parents. Children learn by what we say, do and by what we don't say and do. When a parent decides to homeschool, they have to be intentional about teaching and providing a quality education for their children. I realize that some parents don't feel adequate because they are not teachers by profession but it's amazing how God will give you everything that you need to teach the gifts that He gave you. Where the desire is strong enough, there is no barrier.

Some parents work outside of the home and homeschool while others have homeschooling as their primary job. I refuse to say that parents who are home full time don't work because being a full-time homemaker is work. Homeschooling is an additional responsibility for a parent. Since homeschooling requires a big commitment, it is helpful for parents to have a good support system. When grandparents, godparents and other family members are in agreement with a family's decision to homeschool it is a blessing. There will be times when help is needed to take a child or to pick up a child from an event or activity.

Parents need to have time to step away from homeschooling and to practice self-care. When there are other parents or family members involved, they can help to make sure that parents get a break. Everyone needs to have a break. After our first year of homeschooling, I remember being told by a homeschool evaluator that we had not finished enough work and need to continue working on the curriculum. This was an issue because it was the end of a school year and we all were looking forward to the summer. It was our first year and we worked very hard to have a good first year only to be told you need to do more work in the books. My husband could see that I needed a break and the children too so, we all agreed to take a break. We re-evaluated what we needed to do differently for the next school year so that we could get more work done. The next year we did even better! I said all of that to say, parents have to take care of themselves on the homeschooling journey. You are your child's primary teacher, so it is important that you are in good health. Know your limits and schedule time so that you can be refreshed and renewed. When you take care of yourself, you will be better for your children.

People

THERE IS A FAMOUS QUOTE BY JOHN LYDGATE THAT SAYS; "You can please some of the people all of the time, you can please all of the people some of the time, but you can't please all of the people all of the time." This is so true and a good quote to remember as you start your homeschooling journey. People are something else! You will not be able to please everyone. If you talk to a lot of different people about homeschooling your children, you will get a lot of different responses. Some will be for it and others will have their reasons that they are against homeschooling. You will get advice and suggestions but ultimately, you will need to decide what will work for you, your children and your household.

I was so glad that I prayed and heard a word from God that homeschooling was the educational journey that He was calling me to with my two children. My children asked me about homeschooling them and my husband gave his approval. This was really all the confirmation and consent that I needed; God, my husband and my children were all on board. However, there were people who had questions like why would you want to do that when they can go to a traditional school? What about their socialization skills? How will they graduate from high school? The concerns and the questions were there. However, we persevered. Praise God we didn't let what people thought and said discourage us from homeschooling. Now that my daughter has graduated from homeschool people can see how her homeschooling education worked in her favor. Not only that she was able to go to college and excel. Don't allow the comments and expressions of people stop you from homeschooling if this is what you are planning to do.

Portfolio

HAVE YOU EVER SEEN A STUDENT PROUD OF THEIR WORK? One of the things that a good teacher keeps on her students is a portfolio of their student's work. As a homeschooling parent, you should start compiling samples of your child's work each week. Perhaps one sample from each subject on a weekly basis would help to represent what you have been consistently doing in your home school. A good homeschooling portfolio should provide weekly samples of a child's work, writing, activities, etc. If you have pictures that will document activities, assignments or field trips, this is very helpful to show when being evaluated.

The portfolio is simply a compilation of a student's work. Typically, a three-ring binder that has tabs/dividers for each subject is used. As I collected work samples, I would put three holes in the paper and insert the work in the portfolio. When we first started homeschooling, I would gather samples for the portfolio but as time went on and my children got older, they were responsible for keeping their own portfolio. We made it an exciting project by buying a colored notebook each year and allowing them to create some type of picture to put on the outside cover of the notebook. They would decorate the cover, creatively write their names and the school year.

Keeping an up to date portfolio is also a good form of accountability. I remember having to make sure that my children's work was checked and graded so that we could add it to the portfolio. All the work that was placed in the portfolio was work that was evaluated and graded with feedback. The portfolio is a tool to help you display your child's work, time and skills. Whenever you have a homeschooling review with an evaluator, having a neat, well organized portfolio makes things so much easier.

When I was a homeschool evaluator, I looked for consistency in collecting samples of student's work and work that was dated and graded. If parents were not getting enough time in with their children or children were not spending enough time doing their work, it would show in their portfolio. You cannot produce papers, assignments and schoolwork if you have not been doing anything. This is why it is so important to consistently conduct school and to consistently collect and grade work. Having a portfolio is often recommended and in some cases is required when preparing for a homeschool review.

Planning

"FAILING TO PLAN IS PLANNING TO FAIL." Another key to successful homeschooling is planning. It is so important to start your journey with the end of the school year in mind. First, you select the curriculum that you will use for each subject. Second, when you get the curriculum, you should set a goal for the amount of work you would like to cover and then create a plan to accomplish your goal. Pull out a calendar and map out the work that you would like to cover and the time frame. Create a schedule and stick to it. Plan your work and work your plan. If you make out a great plan and you do not follow it, you probably will not be able to get as much done during the school year.

If necessary, show your plan to someone else as a form of accountability with striving to get the work done. Remember that you are responsible for your child's education and that you want to hear God say well done! Not only do you want to hear God say well done, but the homeschool evaluator as well.

Planning helps to maximize your time from day to day. The days will go by so fast so if you are not being intentional about following your plan, you are likely to waste precious time. Children should be placed on a schedule

The P Principles

with a specific amount of time allocated for each subject. There may be some subjects that require more time based on your child's needs; however, each day there should be a plan. There should be a weekly plan, daily plan and a plan for the overall school year. These plans should work together to get you to your ultimate goal of completing an entire school year of work.

If you plan to incorporate field trips and activities that will take place during school time, you will need to plan so that you can designate another day to get curriculum work done. When your children are old enough, it's a good idea to teach them how to plan so that they can master this skill. When my daughter was in high school, we would sit down at the beginning of the week and look at her curriculum. We would map out what she needed to read, write or even projects that needed to be done. I would let her know what needed to be completed by the end of the week so that we could stay on task with our plan. Having a plan is crucial to you and your child's homeschooling success.

Chapter Seventeen
THE Q PRINCIPLES

Qualified

"Am I qualified to homeschool my child?" You may be asking yourself this question. If so, you are not alone. Many have asked this question. Even though I am a teacher, I still asked myself this question because I don't teach all subjects. I have been accustomed to teaching one subject; not all subjects. When I teach in a traditional school setting, I teach Business. My strength is in reading and writing. I was really concerned about having to teach math and science to my children. I was smart enough to know that I would need to outsource for the subjects that I could not teach. Have you ever been hired for a job that you didn't quite qualify for? Oftentimes what happens is you end up surprising yourself with the skills that you didn't know you had. Whatever skills you need, you end up learning from someone else or someone else comes along and helps you to get the job done. God has a way of qualifying the unqualified. So don't worry about being qualified. I think this question can come to mind with any new job.

The word qualified means that you have been officially recognized as being trained to perform a particular job; you may even be certified and have education in a particular field. This is the general definition of what it means to be qualified. However, when it comes to homeschooling, as I mentioned, God qualifies parents. When a parent has a desire to homeschool their child, God will provide everything that is needed. Much of what is required has already been placed inside of the parent and they just need to be willing to pour out and invest time in their precious gifts from God. God brings things back to your memory so that you can teach your children and what you don't remember, He places other people in your life to help you. There are so many resources available to help a homeschooling parent so you don't have to feel like you must know it all yourself.

As a homeschooling parent, being qualified is more about being willing, available and prepared to homeschool more than anything else. You must be willing to give of yourself, your time, space in your home and your money to be successful. Also available to teach, pour into your child, take field trips and be a good overseer of your children. Being qualified also means that you are prepared to get the job done. You have taken the time to select a curriculum and have a plan to follow. The basic skills of reading and writing are necessary to accomplish the task but these skills are the basics.

Quiet Time

PSALM 46:10 SAYS, "BE STILL AND KNOW THAT I AM GOD . . ." This is a great verse to reflect on when you are a homeschooling parent. One of the things that will enhance you as a parent and as a homeschooling parent is taking time to be quiet. It is a good practice to start your day by being quiet and sitting still. The verse says, "Be still and know that I am God" which means that when we are still there are things that God will reveal, and we will not miss it because we are still. On the other hand, there are some things that we miss because we never take the time to be still and spend some quiet time in the presence of God.

There are things that God wants to say every day but we are too busy or our lives are too noisy to hear Him. Being quiet and being still is a discipline. Each day, I would start my day by having some quiet time. I would be still, read my Bible, pray and sometimes journal. There is something powerful about spending some quiet time with the Lord. When we enter His presence, He restores, refuels and He speaks. He gives us everything we need to make it through the day.

Quiet time is essential for maintaining good mental, physical and emotional health. Parents should teach their children the discipline of being still and quiet to spend time with the Lord. It is a great discipline for them to learn. A good way to implement this is to set a timer for two minutes and announce that we will have two minutes of quiet time before reading our Bible. Try it!

Quitting

MY FORMER PASTOR, THE LATE BISHOP T. TAIT USED TO ALWAYS SAY, "A quitter never wins and a winner never quits." There will be some homeschooling days that may make you want to quit. Perhaps you can allow yourself to quit for the day, but don't quit all together. These are normal feeling, especially if you are homeschooling multiple children. The demands of homeschooling can be overwhelming! I am a witness; God will see you and your family through the homeschooling days. I went from not knowing anything about homeschooling to becoming a homeschool evaluator. Also, I went from just desiring to homeschool for a couple of years to homeschooling through high school. I said all of this to say you don't have to quit. You can finish and finish strong.

Some of the keys to not quitting is staying connected with other people who are homeschooling. If you are homeschooling under an umbrella, that is very helpful and if you have a close friend who happens to also be homeschooling that is even better. It is important to know that you are not alone. You are not the first to homeschool your children and you will not be the last. God will give you everything that you need to successfully homeschool your child. He is faithful!

As a homeschooling parent, I think it is important to teach your child about the significance of not quitting. They will have to work harder in some subjects than others, but they should not quit. A standard should be set to help children learn that just because we are having school at home does not mean that they can quit any time they would like. As much as possible, it is good to stick to the schedule and the amount of time allotted for each subject. We have to help children realize that each day counts towards the goal of learning and completing their curriculum. Don't quit!

Quality Time

ANOTHER ONE OF THE BENEFITS OF HOMESCHOOLING is the quality time that you will spend together. When I say quality, I mean giving your child your undivided attention, listening and observing your child. Finding out as much as you can about how your child thinks, learns and what their interests are, are important to the homeschooling journey. You will certainly get to know your children well as you spend quality time together. If you have one child, you will get one-on-one time every day. However, if you have multiple children you can have quality time with your children all together and you should be intentional about working individually with each child.

Quality time is priceless. There are so many positive things that happen when we spend quality time with our children. You will get to know them better and when you know them, you are more equipped to give them what they need. Something can be provided by you and other things may have to be outsourced. What we may not realize is that all our children will grow up and what will be remembered is the time that we have spent teaching them and training them.

By having quality time with our children, we will build stronger relationships. Many parents are working outside the home and have very little time after work to spend with their children. Therefore, their relationships with their children may not be as strong as they would like.

Chapter Eighteen
THE R PRINCIPLES

Reading

ONE OF THE MOST VALUABLE SKILLS THAT A CHILD CAN LEARN IS HOW TO READ and write. I will address writing in another chapter. Let's focus on the power of just being able to read. Believe it or not, there are kids who make it through the public school system who cannot read and some who don't read very well. I know because I have taught in the public school system for over ten years. You wonder how this happens, but it happens. Reading is fundamental!

When you homeschool your child from the beginning, you get the pleasure of teaching your child how to read. You can give your child a positive experience with books and help to cultivate a love for reading. Taking the time to read to your children every day when they are young helps to foster a good relationship with books. I remember introducing books to my children when they were babies. Even though they could not read, they started by simply learning how to hold a book and turn pages. Their first books were made of plastic and some were made out of cloth. Later they had books that were made out of hard cardboard and then built up to reading books with paper pages.

Reading has many benefits. It allows you to travel to places that you may never physically travel. You can also learn about experiences that you may never actually have but you still have the benefit of learning from the author's experience. Reading helps to stimulate the mind and can help to improve your memory. It is believed that students who read become better writers and develop good vocabulary. Reading is a skill that can be used everywhere you go. Having the freedom of reading and the freedom to choose allows a child to learn about their own interests and passions. When people read about their passions and their own interests, it's easy to lose track of time. Whenever we took a road trip or we were going somewhere that would require us to have wait time, I would tell my children to grab a book for the ride. It's a good habit to read when you have wait time. Due to technology, many of our kids have electronic devices and use their wait time to play a game or play on an application. There are books that can be read electronically and there are also applications that will read to your children. Although electronic games may be more appealing to our children, as parents, we should keep encouraging the power of reading a book. Good readers become good leaders!

Record Keeping

GOOD TEACHERS AND GOOD PARENTS HAVE TO KEEP GOOD RECORDS! No matter how good of a memory you have, there are some things that you will need to write down. You will need to store grades and write observations about your child's work. This is especially true when you have multiple children. You can't rely on your memory to recall every assignment and grade given. Good record keeping allows you to have evidence of how a student has performed during the school year. I always felt like other people are questioning whether I am really teaching my children and whether they are actually learning. Therefore, I made sure that I kept good records of everything that we were doing so that I could always have proof that we were working consistently and that my children were learning something.

Good records make life easier whenever you have a homeschool review and if you happen to have to send your child back into a traditional school, you will have some proof of the type of work that your child is capable of doing. Some of the things that you should keep records of are their weekly work assignments, writing samples, vocabulary words and as I mentioned before, try to collect something from each subject at least once a week. In addition, it is also important to keep good attendance records. You should keep track of the number of days that school is in session and make a note of the days that you will not have school. Students need to have so many hours in school in order to have a complete school year. Good records will help you to monitor your child's progress throughout the school year. It's a good feeling to be able to see the progress of your student.

Respect

AS PARENTS WE MUST TEACH OUR CHILDREN RESPECT. Respect for God, respect for you as a parent, respect for themselves and for others. They should learn what it means to show respect and how to treat people. If we don't teach our children respect, how will they know? How we allow them to talk to us will often be the way that they talk to others. As a teacher in the public school system, I have found that some students will come to school and say disrespectful things because they are allowed to say them at home. Children who are respectful go a lot further in life than children who are disrespectful.

Parents can model respect with the way that they talk to their spouse in front of their children. One day I saw this little girl talking to her father in such a disrespectful way; then I realized that the daughter was only saying what she heard her mother say. Respect should be modeled and taught. People don't mind working with children who are well-mannered and respectful. Everyone deserves to be treated with respect. One of the things that will put a bad taste in my mouth is when a child disrespects an adult. A child really needs to learn to stay in a child's place.

Part of a child learning to respect their parents is learning to obey their wishes. The Bible tells children to obey their parents in the Lord for this is right (Ephhesians 6:1). When you have a high level of respect for your parents, you will do what they say and respect their wishes (this of course means that they are not asking their children to do something immoral or unethical).

We should also teach our children the importance of respecting those who are in authority: leaders, police officers and their elders. Yes, we should treat everyone with respect but there are some special people that children need to be sure to respect. I think we should teach our children that if you are somewhere and the seats are limited, as the younger person, they should give up their seat for an elder out of respect for the elderly. If we are walking into a building and there is someone behind us we should teach our children to respect the person behind you enough to hold the door. It's little things like this that mean a lot. How would a child know to do this? Respect must be taught!

Review

THANK GOD FOR HOMESCHOOLING REVIEWS! A homeschooling review is a meeting that can take place at any time during the school year but normally takes place at the beginning or the end. Most people have at least two reviews a school year and sometimes more. The review can be in person and a follow up review may be over the phone. If you are homeschooling under a particular state, there may be a state representative who schedules to meet with you and your child to evaluate your homeschooling. If you are under a homeschool umbrella, you will have your review from someone under the homeschool umbrella. In both cases, the person conducting the review will look for certain things. For example, your child should have a portfolio (Notebook) with consistent samples of weekly work. The work should be graded, dated and neatly organized so that the reviewer can easily see what your child has been doing.

The homeschool review was generally no longer than 30 minutes to one hour. It depends on the amount of work that you and your child share. Also, some reviewers ask more questions than others. Having a homeschool review in a timely fashion can be very helpful. A good reviewer will tell you things that you are doing well, things that you are not doing well and give suggestions for change. Oftentimes the reviewer is someone experienced in homeschooling and can offer a wealth of information, ideas and suggestions. I always appreciated having time with the person conducting the review. When you homeschool under an umbrella, they will assign someone to give you a review a couple of times during the school year. However, when you homeschool under the state there may be fewer reviews depending on each state's requirements.

The R Principles

Having a review also protects you. If you are not on the right track, the reviewer can observe and share information to help you to get on the right track. They will let you know if you are not getting enough work done with your child or if there is something that you need to do differently. I remember when I worked as a homeschool reviewer, there were some parents who seemed to avoid scheduling the review. In each of those cases, it was usually because the parent was not on top of their job with the homeschooling. Their children were home but there was little structure and little work being done. This was a problem. Reviews don't go well if you have little to show and very little work has been done for a grading period. I was always told, "People do what you inspect, not always what you expect." This means that we all need a form of accountability. We need to know that someone will be checking on us to see what and how we are doing. Having a review is a way of getting you and your child's work inspected. Of course, if your child is young, you will prepare for the review by gathering your child's work. However, if your child is older, your job as a parent is to oversee your child and make sure that they have everything ready to present. Your child should have their portfolio full of consistent assignments in each subject that have been graded and dated. Having a great review is the goal!

Chapter Nineteen
THE S PRINCIPLES

Schedule

IF YOU WANT TO MAXIMIZE EACH HOMESCHOOLING DAY, YOU MUST HAVE A schedule. We all know that time flies; however, when you are not intentional about what you want to accomplish each day, the days and the time will fly by and before you know it, a quarter is ending and you have not accomplished what you wanted to accomplish. Having a schedule that you will stick to is essential for successful homeschooling. There are so many things that need to be done as you educate your children, so it is important to map out exactly what you plan to do each day.

SUBJECT/ACTIVITY	TIME
Wake up, Get Dressed, Have breakfast	7:30 – 8:30
Devotions/Bible	8:30 – 9:15
Math	9:30 – 10:15
Language Arts	10:30 – 11:15
History	11:30 – 12:00
Lunch	12:00 – 1:00
Science	1:00 – 1:45
Extracurricular/Gym	2:00 – 2:45

This is a sample of how a day can go. You may decide that on Mondays and Wednesdays you will have one schedule and on Tuesdays and Thursdays you will have another schedule. Fridays were our light day. Sometimes we would go on a field trip on Fridays. You can be flexible with your schedule and make changes as necessary. The important thing is to have a schedule and try your best to stick to it. It is important to have a schedule of how many days a week you will spend on each subject that is required. If not, you can go the entire school year and not have enough curriculum covered in a particular subject.

Having a schedule is also helpful for making sure that you are spending adequate time in each subject. If you are homeschooling and not spending enough time in each subject this will hinder your successful completion of the curriculum. Be sure to sit down and write out a schedule. You need to have a schedule for you and for your homeschooler. Teach your child how to make a schedule and how to follow it. They need to learn time management skills and be responsible for allocating a certain amount of time for each subject.

While scheduling, be sure to allocate some time for yourself each day. Even if it is only 10 minutes. I always scheduled my time with the Lord before I started homeschooling. On any given day, I would schedule phone calls, appointments, time to cook meals, etc. Most of the time when we set a schedule, we would stick to it. Scheduling is just a way for me to make sure that I get in the things that are important for the day.

Socialization

"WHAT ABOUT SOCIALIZATION?" This is one of the most common questions that I was asked by people who discovered that I was homeschooling. I think when you say that you are homeschooling, people envision your child being left alone having no interaction with other kids. In addition, they think that your child will not be able to interact with other children and communicate well. Just like anything else, there is a right way and wrong way to do something. I don't agree with taking your kids out of a traditional school environment to totally keep them away from interacting with other people and isolating them. As a homeschooling parent you can determine how you want your homeschool to be and make it happen. I wanted my children to be well rounded and exposed to socializing with a variety of people from their peers to adults.

Parents who successfully homeschool are intentional about creating opportunities for their children to get in socialization time. There are many ways to incorporate socialization into your homeschooling time.

First, invite other homeschoolers over for playdates or study dates. When you are teaching a topic that can benefit others, invite other homeschoolers to share. We were involved with a homeschooling umbrella that offered classes twice a week for homeschoolers. The classes are divided into various age groups and subjects. Twice a week my children would get out of the house to have classes with other children.

Second, attend church on a regular basis. We go to church every Sunday and our children have been used to going since before they were born. We attend church as a family and then there are various activities for the children to participate in. The activities are generally for a specific age group. For example, Sunday School, Youth Ministry, Kids Magazine and Dance for my daughter. Some of the activities meet once a week, and some once a month. However, this is a good way to get your child involved and socializing with their peers.

Third, sign up for volunteer work in the community. One of our most popular places was to sign up to serve with the Central Union Missions in Washington, D. C. My kids and I helped to serve the senior citizens. We live in Maryland but it was nice to take the trips to D.C. to serve. It gave my children a different perspective.

Fourth, wherever you go to places like the store, depending on the age of your child, you can give them responsibilities to interact with the salesperson, the bank teller or someone on the phone, etc.

Fifth, there are so many classes and sports activities in the area that you can sign your child up to take. My children took gym classes with other children under the Maryland Park and Planning Program. Check out your local community to see what they offer. My son played football with a local community team. My daughter took classes at the local community college during her senior year. She socialized with students her age, older students and adults.

The last thing that I want to say is that you should teach your children how to socialize and practice by having people over in your own home. Teach your children how to treat guests, how to smile and look people in the eyes, how to talk and be hospitable.

Sports

THERE ARE SOME KIDS WHO LOVE SPORTS and want to be a part of a team. Homeschooling should not be the reason that your child is not involved in sports. Physical Education is a required subject and there are various options for children to participate. My son loved the game of football and he was so happy when we found a football team in our community. I will never forget that day. My husband was driving down the street and noticed a sign that said a football team was starting and that they practice several days during the week. He saw a number posted, and I called to inquire. I called in the evening and the coach answered. I shared that my son was homeschooled but wanted to play football. He said can you get him here now? I told Ahmad that the coach was waiting for his arrival at the practice. He was so excited! He changed his clothes and I drove him to his first tackle football practice. This ended up being a great outlet for my son, and he really enjoyed playing the game. The coaches were nice and were a positive influence on my son (this is important because the boys spent so much time at practice and being around the coaches). He met other boys his age and developed friendships. The team ended up being very successful and made it all the way to Florida for two years straight to play competitive games. The team played very well, and we traveled to see them play. Being involved as a homeschooler was great. Each boy came from different schools to be a part of this community team; therefore, it wasn't like my son was an outsider. He was the only one who was homeschooled but this was never an issue because all of the boys came from different schools.

My son had a great experience getting involved with the local football team and really enjoyed himself.

The S Principles

Another option to getting your child involved with sports is through a local recreation center or sports and learning complex. They normally offer classes in various sports and you can sign your child up for a sport that will fit your schedule. You do have to be careful about signing you and your child up for sports activities and events. You can make yourself too busy and then it becomes a problem because your children aren't able to finish enough of their schoolwork if they are always on the go. So you have to be careful not to over commit to being involved in things that will take you all away from being able to get their work done. I have heard homeschooling moms say that they have experienced times where they had their children involved in so many activities that they were spending too much time on the go. When you have to leave the house every day to go to this practice or that activity, it can be challenging to get schoolwork done. So there needs to be a good balance of time for schoolwork and time for sports and activities.

There are many benefits of having your child involved in sports and physical activities. My son happened to enjoy football and my daughter enjoyed her years of being involved in dance. I believe they both learned valuable lessons by being involved in sports. The following are a few lessons. First, it helped them both to get regular exercise. Exercise is important and when kids get it in, they are less likely to be overweight. Children who are homeschooled are more likely to spend more time learning in the home; therefore, parents need to be intentional about allowing them time to play games, sports or to physically move their bodies. Second, being involved with sports teaches children teamwork. Ahmad learned how to work together with his teammates and together they made a successful football team in the community. Ciara learned lessons by participating in dance. Both of my children developed stronger relationships with people that they met on the journey of participating in a sports activity. Third, children learn time management skills when participating in sports. They have to manage their time well to get their work done before they can practice. When Ciara's dance group participated in the Christmas play, there were several late-night rehearsals. She had to get all of her schoolwork done in a timely fashion before going to the rehearsals. Ahmad learned how to get his work done and make it to practice just about every day. Fourth, participating in sports can help in teaching children leadership skills. Oftentimes children are given leadership roles while participating on a team.

State Supervision

AS I PREVIOUSLY MENTIONED, EACH STATE HAS DIFFERENT REQUIREMENTS for homeschoolers. However, it is a known fact that children starting at the age of 5-16 must attend a public school on a regular basis or receive their education through another option that is equally thorough. Homeschooling can be that option but parents must be supervised. If you are planning to homeschool, one of the first things you should know is what your state regulations are and what they offer for homeschoolers. Most states provide some type of supervision to homeschooling parents. The expectation is that a homeschooling parent would be connected with a state-approved supervisor, a bona-fide church organization or connect with a local school that assigns a school teacher to help oversee the work of the homeschooler.

Having supervision from the state usually means that the state provides enrollment conferences for parents to attend. These conferences help to educate the parent on what is required and expected as a homeschooler. Having supervision also means that the state wants to review the textbooks/curriculum and lesson plans that are being used to educate your child. Although as a parent, you get to select the educational tools that your child will use, when you have state supervision, someone will be checking to see what you are using. The state will also make annual homeschool visits to check to see how you and your child are doing as a homeschooling family. They want to make sure that the child is being educated according to their state requirements. The goal is to make sure that your homeschooler is thoroughly educated.

When I first started homeschooling, I met a parent who was being supervised by the state and parents who selected a homeschooling umbrella at a local church. I was told that the state does not visit as often as someone who provides supervision under a homeschooling umbrella at a church. Therefore, I decided to connect with a homeschooling umbrella. The first two years we homeschooled under a local homeschooling umbrella that was very close to my house. After the first two years, we joined an umbrella under the church that we attend. Having good supervision was very important to me because I wanted to make sure that I wasn't doing my child a dis-service in any way. Having good supervision provided a source of accountability for me to do what I needed to do.

Chapter Twenty
THE T PRINCIPLES

Technology

THE USE OF TECHNOLOGY HAS MADE A WONDERFUL IMPACT ON HOMESCHOOLING! Many of my friends who were homeschooling twenty years ago or more did not have all the things that are offered by way of technology. Technology offers so many tools to help homeschooling parents educate their children. The use of the internet and online classes provide learning opportunities for all students. Technology allows students to research any subject, define any word, incorporate music, see visuals and watch a video within seconds. I know this can be both good and bad, but let's just focus on the benefit of that and what it means to education. Parents who want to homeschool can really enhance their children's education by using these tools.

Technology enhanced many of the lessons that my children learned throughout their years of homeschooling. I can remember a history lesson that my son was learning about the Sydney Opera House in Australia because we were able to research it, see a current picture of it, learn about its architecture and how it is one of the world's greatest attractions. It's one of the places that I would love to see in person because of the information that was provided online. There were so many lessons that were brought to life because of the use of technology in our homeschool classroom.

Technology also provides the opportunity for students to learn by being a part of virtual classrooms with endless possibilities. There are virtual programs that provide education for grades K-12 in many states. The virtual programs bring the classroom to students in their homes and offer a high-level education with instructors who are educators. The virtual programs are a blessing to many homeschoolers because it is offered by public school systems and it is free. These programs are easy to use and are offered to students in various states. Parents, students and teachers can connect by way of a virtual classroom. Students can even connect with other students around the world by way of technology. These opportunities help to enrich any child's education. These programs are accredited and even offer college preparation courses. Parents can be assigned a counselor to connect with to help select the courses for their children.

The use of technology in the classroom makes learning limitless. There are really no excuses for a child not being able to learn successfully at home when technology is used. Today new technologies make homeschooling easier and provide wonderful opportunities to students and parents. Although technology is great, many agree that it does not replace the human touch. Since so many children have been forced to become distance learners during the pandemic of 2020, parents and students have begun to appreciate the significance of having a teacher and being able to learn with other students in person.

Testing

WHEN I WAS A STUDENT IN SCHOOL, I didn't like when it was time for a test. Testing brought a level of anxiety especially for subjects that I didn't think I was good in. Since math was a challenging subject for me, I did not like when it was time for a test. However, the test was a good indicator for the teacher to know how much I understood about what was being taught. When you are homeschooling, it is a good idea to test your students at the end of a chapter or unit to see how much of the information has been retained. Most of the homeschooling curriculum have tests already embedded in the chapters after so much information has been taught. When you give your student a test, it is a good idea to check the test as soon as possible and give immediate feedback. Based on how well the student performs, you can determine whether you should move on to the next lesson or if you need to review and stay on the current lesson longer.

Tests are good indicators for what needs to be done as well as how well your child is learning the information. I was very happy to know that the homeschooling umbrella provided a standardized test every year for each grade level. I signed up to have both of my children tested to see if there were any areas that needed to be worked on and to see if they were working on their grade level. Standardized tests are normally developed to give students and parents an idea of a child's academic skills and abilities. There are several different tests and once your child takes a standardized test the company giving the test can compare your child with other children who are the same age or in the same grade.

I would feel some kind of way when my children took the standardized test. I think it's because in the back of my mind I felt if they don't test well, I must not be doing something right. I also felt if their scores were not good it could be an indicator that they need to go back to a traditional school setting. Therefore, I was a bit nervous about seeing the results. I never mentioned these feelings to my children but these were in my secret thoughts. Thankfully, each time that they were tested, they both did well. In some areas they were above their grade levels. What a blessing! Allowing your children to take standardized tests is a good way to learn more about your child. I want to encourage parents to see testing as a helpful tool and not as a threat.

Some states require standard testing for all students. It is important to have formal assessments to see how children are doing. Since children will have to take a standardized test at some point in their life, it is good for parents to teach test strategies. Basic things like making sure you bubble in all of the circle, reading the entire question, looking for cues, pacing yourself based on the time given, finding out if it is okay to take an educated guess and answering all of the questions, etc. If possible, do some research on the type of test that your child will be given so that you can adequately prepare. Also, there are books in the library, there is information online and there are classes that your child can take to help prepare for certain standardized tests. Preparation is the key!

Transcript

ONE OF THE CONCERNS THAT I HAD ABOUT HOMESCHOOLING my daughter through high school was having a transcript that was acceptable for colleges to view. I knew that my daughter would be going to college, and I did not want to do a disservice by not having the proper transcript. When your children are younger, there is less emphasis on the transcript. However, when your child is in high school and preparing for college, more emphasis is placed on the transcript. A transcript is a very important document that provides an academic record of all of the courses taken and the grades that were earned throughout your years of school. Colleges look at transcripts to help determine a student's ability to perform in college. The transcript is a major piece in the college application process.

When you really want a college to evaluate your transcript you should send an official transcript for review. In a traditional school, the guidance counseling office is normally the go to place for official transcripts. The office will send a sealed authorized copy directly to the college of your choice for a small fee. As a homeschooling parent, I wondered how I would do this since my child is no longer in a traditional school setting. Later, I learned that when you are under a homeschooling umbrella, you submit your child's grades and they provide a transcript to the colleges of your choice for a fee. If you are homeschooling and you are not under an umbrella, you can create your own transcript. However, you need to be very professional in the way that you present your child's records and you should do a little research on the do's and don'ts with turning in an official transcript. You will need to include the basic information such as; a list of the courses taken, the number of credits received from each course, the student's grade and their cumulative grade point average. Some high school transcripts include additional information such as disciplinary records, awards or honors and standardized test scores. It is very important that the information is correct. I personally did not want to take on this responsibility, so I was glad that the homeschooling umbrella provided this service.

The T Principles

Travel

AS AN EDUCATOR BY PROFESSION, one of the things that I have noticed is that the thing that often makes one student more knowledgeable than another is exposure. If one child has actually traveled and seen fifty states firsthand, they are likely to have more knowledge than a child who has never left their state before. Traveling allows students to learn and experience things that they may have never seen before. There is something about going to a place and experiencing the culture, the weather, seeing sights and talking to the people that allows children to learn in a different way.

It doesn't matter if you have traveled by car, bus, train or plane; each method provides a different learning experience. Children can learn something different by traveling on each. There were times when we took a road trip and pointed out various sights as we passed through different states. Taking a trip using public transportation can be fun because children learn what it is like to travel with a large group of people. There are so many lessons to learn just from traveling.

One of the things that I really enjoyed about our homeschooling days was taking field trips. We took local trips in the community and trips to places in D.C., Maryland and Virginia. We visited museums, restaurants, stores and went to various events to simply be exposed to different things. Each trip brought a different lesson. Our most memorable trip was our cross-country trip on the train to California. We left on a Monday and arrived on a Thursday. It was amazing! We stopped in different states, experienced different time zones, met people from all over the world and experienced taking an Uber for the first time in California. While we were there, we were blessed with tickets to attend the BET awards. We saw celebrities and experienced the live BET Awards show that comes on television. My children made a list of all the places and restaurants that they had heard about in California, and we spent our trip visiting those places. When it was time to go home, we took a plane back. It was truly an experience to remember, all because we traveled.

Chapter Twenty-One

THE U PRINCIPLES

Umbrella

THANK GOD FOR A GOOD UMBRELLA! JUST AS A GOOD UMBRELLA KEEPS YOU covered in the rain and helps to protect you from getting soaked, a homeschool umbrella covers families who homeschool. Being a part of a homeschool umbrella means that you have someone to oversee your homeschooling journey. The umbrella is an organization or a school that helps to make sure that homeschooling families are meeting the requirements of the state.

There is normally a fee to join a homeschool umbrella and the fee varies based on the services that you select. Homeschool umbrellas provide oversight only for one fee and provide oversight along with co-op for another fee. The co-op is when you are given the option to meet with other families who are homeschooling. Children can benefit by having activities, classes, service work, projects, field trips, arts and crafts and social time with other children. We selected the oversight and the co-op classes and it provided a nice balance for my children! We selected classes that children needed to take for state requirements and they went to the classes twice a week. It was good for them to have two consistent days that they left the house. They were in a learning environment with other students and were assigned work from other teachers. On Monday, Wednesday and Fridays we would work from home and on Tuesday and Thursdays they would go to co-op classes provided by the homeschool umbrella.

Being a part of a homeschool umbrella made homeschooling more doable for me. I needed the structure and accountability. Another advantage of being under a homeschool umbrella that I previously mentioned, is that they provide you with official transcripts for your children.

In the seven years of homeschooling, I was a part of two different homeschool umbrellas. The first umbrella I selected was all about convenience. It was the closest one to my home. After two years, I decided to join the umbrella under my church because it was a more warm and friendly environment. We knew many of the homeschooling families and we felt at home since the co-op met at our church. It was important for me to feel connected as well as for my children. Joining the umbrella at my church was a great move for us. We were well supported through the homeschooling journey. We ended our homeschooling journey under the umbrella with my daughter graduating from high school and participating in a special graduation specifically for homeschoolers. I highly recommend being a part of a homeschool umbrella!

Understanding

HOMESCHOOLING GIVES PARENTS A BETTER UNDERSTANDING of their children. When you are working closely with your child day in and day out, you get to observe things about your child that you may not have known. You get to see their strengths and their weaknesses. In addition, you will learn how they learn best. When you have an understanding of how your child thinks and learns you will be better able to educate them.

Once you understand how your child learns, you will be able to select curriculum and resources that will be best for your child's learning style. Children can learn in a variety of ways and as a parent you want to select what's best. If possible, it is good to spend some time reviewing the curriculum before you purchase it to be sure that it will provide what you need. After you purchase the curriculum, you should review the material to make sure that you have an understanding of what is expected and how much time your child needs to spend on it to get it done in a timely fashion.

Having an understanding of what is expected of you as a homeschooling parent is important. It took me a minute to process the fact that many of the things that I was relying on the school to do, I now had to do myself. For example, selecting the best curriculum, grading my child's school work and teaching all of the subjects were new responsibilities.

Don't expect for someone else to understand your reasons for homeschooling your child. When God places the desire in your heart, do what needs to be done to get an understanding of what homeschooling is all about and do it! Sometimes I found myself hoping that others would understand my why. It wasn't really for them to understand. You have to do what you feel is best for you and your child whether others understand or not.

Underestimate

NEVER UNDERESTIMATE THE POWER OF GOD when you choose to homeschool! The Lord exceeded my expectations with how He made ways, opened doors and provided everything that we needed to homeschool successfully. When I think of the goodness of Jesus and all that He did on our homeschooling journey, my soul cries out hallelujah! I thank God.

Even though I am an educator by profession, I underestimated my ability to homeschool and certainly was apprehensive about going all the way through high school. I learned that it really wasn't about my ability. I really believe that this was the journey that God had me to take and He promised to be with me every step of the way. Allow me to tell of His goodness! He provided everything that I wanted to homeschool my children. I wanted a classroom for us to go into every day, and the Lord provided. I wanted a desk, lockers and everything that would give them a feel of being in school; the Lord provided. I wasn't sure about which curriculum I should select and He gave me guidance so that I could make the best choice. I am not good in math or science, so I didn't know how I would get these subjects taught. The Lord provided a math tutor who worked with my daughter until she finished high school. Her science classes were taught under a homeschooling co-op that I didn't know anything about but the Lord had a friend to share the information. I was concerned about continuing to homeschool my daughter through high school because of all the requirements, but God provided everything that we needed.

I believe my daughter had a well-rounded experience on her homeschooling journey. We may have initially underestimated what this experience would be like but God! God enriched the homeschooling journey and showed himself mighty! We were able to successfully homeschool my daughter through high school and she was accepted into the university of her choice.

University

ONE OF MY BIGGEST FEARS WITH HOMESCHOOLING my daughter through high school was will she be prepared to go to a university? I wasn't sure if I could adequately prepare her for college but then I thought about all the things that I needed to know to be prepared when I was going to college. I remember getting prepared by making good grades throughout my high school years. The counselors did talk about having a good transcript. Therefore, as I prepared my daughter, my concern was that her grades were good and that her transcript was prepared in a professional way. The first part really wasn't a concern because Ciara has always had her own desire to make good grades. She was making good grades before we began homeschooling. I attended a workshop on preparing your homeschooler for college and learned the significance of having the transcript prepared in a professional way so this was my concern. To my surprise, there was no need for me to worry because the homeschool umbrella produced the college transcripts as a service to all the seniors. There were other things that needed to be done in preparation for college and I just wanted to make sure that we did everything we needed to do.

She took the SAT and ACT tests to prepare. We bought books and she read things online to prepare for the tests. We made some visits to different universities and took tours to get an idea of what she should look for in a college. After taking a few college tours, Ciara selected a University that she wanted to attend. When it was time to apply, Ciara spent time preparing her college essay, completed the application and then sent it electronically. She had one university in mind and decided that she would only apply to that one. I know counselors normally recommend that students apply to at least 3 or 4 colleges but Ciara had her mind set on one and was confident that she would get in. Praise God she got accepted into her first and only choice of college.

One of the things that I believe helped to prepare Ciara for taking courses at the university was taking courses at the community college first. I don't believe she was confident about her ability until she took classes at the community college and did very well. Also, homeschooling requires a lot of discipline and good study habits. The same discipline and study habits that Ciara used as a homeschooler also helped to prepare her for doing her work on the university level. She was used to making a schedule for herself, allocating a certain amount of time to get her work done in each subject and daily check lists to be sure that she got all her work done. Discipline is one of the keys to succeeding at a university and Ciara has demonstrated that she has mastered the keys. Homeschoolers (like any other students) can be successfully prepared to get into college, maintain good grades and graduate from a University.

Chapter Twenty-Two
THE *V* PRINCIPLES

Vacation

EVERYONE NEEDS A BREAK AT SOME POINT! WHEN YOU ARE A HOMESCHOOLING parent, you rarely get a break. I remember feeling like I am always ON. On as mother, wife, teacher and leader. There is always something that needs to be done. Having a break, getting away or actually traveling somewhere for a vacation is necessary. It is important to step away and be refreshed. I have previously mentioned several benefits of homeschooling. Another great benefit is simply being able to take a vacation at any time of the year. You don't have to schedule your vacation around the same time as traditional school children; you can plan a vacation when the majority are back in school if you like. Whenever you schedule a vacation, you can adjust your homeschooling schedule so that the work will get done in a timely fashion. Taking a vacation with your children can also be a learning experience but if you really want a break, you will need to promise not to be in "teacher" mode while on vacation.

Wherever you go, you can create an educational lesson around your trip. You can have your children learn facts about the place before they go; this way they will be well informed before they arrive. Also, they can work before the vacation so that they actually get a break while they are away. Now you may not want to do any official work on your vacation but everything is a learning experience. You don't have to say anything about it while you are on vacation but as you spend time sightseeing or riding in the car, your children are learning. Some things you may need to point out or share but know that they are learning even while on vacation. Take lots of pictures to document your vacation and the things that you experienced. After your trip, it is good to reflect on the trip and everything that you experienced. Have your children write about their vacation.

Some parents may be able to get a vacation without their children; if so, you can use the trip as a time to totally relax and get refreshed. I know it is challenging to take trips without your children especially when they are young. My husband and I managed to get a few weekend getaways in without our children. The biggest concern has always been childcare, but we were blessed to have family to care for them while we were gone. Having time to focus on yourself and your spouse can be just what you need to come back motivated for the next school year.

If you are not able to travel away from home, be sure to plan a staycation. A staycation is a vacation too. It just means that you spend your time at home and plan some day trips or visit some local attractions. Since we homeschooled on one income, we weren't always able to have a vacation far away from home. It doesn't matter if you have a vacation or staycation; it is important to have some form of a break or get away to be refreshed.

Validate

IT'S A GOOD FEELING TO BE VALIDATED. I needed validation from time to time to let me know that I was doing what I needed to be doing to successfully homeschool my child. On the other hand, as my daughter moved into high school, she needed to be validated on the fact that she really was a good student and that she was getting everything that she needed. I think there was always a little doubt. I often wondered, "Are we doing everything correctly? Is there anything else that I should be doing to make sure that my daughter is not lacking or missing anything?" I believe my daughter had the same concerns.

However, each time that we had a homeschool review and were evaluated, we were validated. We were encouraged to know that Ciara was getting what she needed academically. In addition to her academics, God made sure that Ciara got what she needed socially, mentally, emotionally and physically.

The next level of validation that we both received was when Ciara went to college. One day out of the blue, she sent us a text just to say thank you! What a blessing this was to me and my husband because we believe that she had a moment in college which helped her to see that she was blessed with a wonderful high school homeschool journey. One of the things that really helped to validate the fact that we did what we were supposed to do is seeing our daughter go through college being on the Dean's list from start to finish. What a validation to know that we obviously did something right! To God be the glory!

Variety

VARIETY IS THE SPICE OF LIFE! Yes, there is never a dull moment when you have variety. Homeschooling allows parents to do a variety of things with their children and to provide a variety of experiences. The great thing about it is that your children can learn from everything that you expose them to. There are a variety of things that you can do and incorporate into your child's education.

Each year that you homeschool, you should decide what you would like to focus on and make a list of things that you would like for your children to experience. For example, participating in community service projects, learning to help others, cooking, participating in sports, being a part of a ministry or activities in the church and traveling. There are so many things that can be incorporated into your homeschool.

There are a variety of homeschooling organizations that you can connect with; all you have to do is use the internet to search for homeschooling organizations. Many of the organizations provide different services that you need on your homeschooling journey. There is help from choosing the curriculum you will use, providing support groups, having accountability and even in having legal help if necessary. Almost every state provides a variety of options for homeschooling. As the homeschooling community has grown, there are more and more options for homeschooling.

Homeschooling can be an exciting journey! As a homeschooling parent you can enrich your child's educational journey by networking and providing a variety of experiences. Each year, homeschooling can be exciting for both you and your child by adding variety.

Vocabulary

HAVE YOU LEARNED A NEW WORD LATELY? One of the things that I strongly believe is that children should be learning vocabulary on a regular basis. Each week there should be some words or a word that you are intentional about teaching, focusing on and incorporating into your lessons. Children should be challenged to learn words and the meaning of different words on a daily basis. When children are younger and just learning to read, we are more likely to introduce new words because almost every word is new. However, as children get older in middle and high school they still should be learning and increasing their vocabulary.

Most curricula have vocabulary words highlighted in each subject. Children can learn vocabulary in Bible, language arts, science, history and even in math. As your child goes from one lesson to the next, they should be increasing their vocabulary. As the children learn various words, there should be a time where they learn the definitions and are tested to see if they have comprehended the word and its meaning.

When children start learning words, it is a good time to introduce the dictionary (an actual hardback book) or a dictionary online. Introducing new words on a regular basis and teaching children to be quick to define words that they are not familiar with is a good way to increase your child's vocabulary. I see it as a discipline and the more you do it, children will increase their vocabulary. Take time to read with your children or listen to them read; when they come across words they are not familiar with, you should stop and define the word. Defining the word and looking at how it is used in a sentence is a good way to learn new words. As you are going places, taking trips or even engaging in various conversations, children will hear and come across various new words but it takes intentionality to learn the word, its meaning and how to properly use the word. At one point, we would discuss the word of the day because when you use dictionary.com the word of the day will pop up. Depending upon the age of your child you share the word of the day and learn the definition.

Remember, vocabulary is critical to your child's success. It is so important to incorporate vocabulary words in your child's daily learning and be sure that they comprehend the meaning of the word. Studies show that vocabulary growth is directly related to school achievement. Often- times a child's vocabulary is used to predict their ability to learn to read. Developing your child's vocabulary helps them to think and learn about the world. When children have extensive vocabulary, they are likely to improve in all areas of communication such as listening, speaking, reading and writing.

Chapter Twenty-Three
THE *W* PRINCIPLES

Why?

WHAT IS YOUR "WHY?" EVERY PARENT WHO DECIDES TO HOMESCHOOL SHOULD know their "why." What is your reason for homeschooling your child? It is important to think about and know your reason because there will be days when you will have to remind yourself of the reason you decided to homeschool.

I remember having some days where I asked myself, "Why am I doing this?" There were days when I felt like this is too much work and I am responsible for too much. I would ask myself, "Why am I putting myself through this when I could send my child to a school where they will do all of this for me?" All I can say is I know that homeschooling was what God called me to do. It all started with both of my kids asking me to homeschool them. Although they asked, I believe that it was all a part of God's plan. I answered the call to homeschool both of my children. However, I believe God later had a different route for Ahmad and wanted me to continue homeschooling Ciara. For whatever reason, my husband and I felt that Ciara was supposed to have a different journey. We did not pull her out of a traditional school setting because of any issues or problems; it was simply because God said so. We honestly homeschooled because this was the journey that God had specifically for Ciara. Each child is different and it is important to seek God for the best direction for each of your children. I realize that in most households it is one way or the other. However, God allowed us to homeschool both children together for three years and then we decided that another route was best for Ahmad. I believe that he benefited from the three-year journey of being homeschooled; then God made a way for him to return to his former school.

There will be some days where homeschooling is challenging and demanding. When you have this kind of day, you may question yourself and every now and then someone else may even question you. It is important to know your why so that you can remind yourself of why you are doing what you are doing.

Work

THIS PRINCIPLE RAISES TWO QUESTIONS IN MY MIND. First, "Are you willing to do the work required to homeschool your child?" Homeschooling does require the parent to do a lot of work but you can do it! Philippians 4:13 tells us that we can do all things through Christ who strengthens us. It is necessary to do the work and remember that you are not alone. God will be with you every step of the way. He will lead, guide and provide everything that you need to get the work done.

Second, "Can a parent work outside the home and successfully homeschool their child at the same time?" YES! I have seen it done but there has to be a strong support system from the other parent, grandparents, friends of the family or family member. During the beginning of my homeschooling journey, I did not work outside the home. I dedicated my time to getting our school off to a strong start. As time went on, I worked part time. During the years that I homeschooled, I met parents who had different working scenarios.

I met one mom who was a single parent who homeschooled both of her children. She was a nurse by profession and somehow, she was able to work from home most of the time. When she had to go in, she had a support system that watched her children but for the most part they were with her. They took online homeschooling courses and she made sure that their work was done based on the demands of the teachers they had online. At the time, I was their homeschool evaluator so I met with the mom and the children. I was so happy to see that their mom was doing a great job as a single parent and that her children were successfully being homeschooled. All of their work was well documented.

One of my good friends homeschooled two of her three children through their high school years while she was working a demanding full-time job. However, her husband and her mother were very much involved with the homeschooling journey. Her children took classes at the homeschooling co-op, online and took courses at the local community college. Her husband and mother would often get her children back and forth to their classes and she would oversee their work in the evenings. She would also communicate with their teachers as necessary. Both of her children graduated from high school and went on to college. One has graduated with a degree in Accounting and the other will also graduate. Both are doing well!

In closing, there are different ways to make homeschooling work for your family. The traditional way of homeschooling consisted of two parents. The father would normally be the parent who was working and the mother would be home full time homeschooling. However, today, not every parent is able to homeschool without working outside the home. Since the cost of living is very high in most areas, parents are often trying to work a job outside the home and homeschool. Homeschooling is definitely a job within it itself and it is really demanding so if you don't have to take on a job outside the home, don't do it. However, if you must work outside the home, be sure to have a strong support system so that you can work and successfully homeschool your child.

Worry

I KNOW THE BIBLE TELLS US NOT TO WORRY, but I think every parent worries about their child at some point. As a homeschooling parent, I found myself worrying about the homeschooling journey. I had all kinds of thoughts like: Do I know enough to homeschool my child? Is my child getting everything that she needs? Is there anything that we missed teaching that may hurt my child later? What will life in college be like for my child? What if this happens or what if that happens? For example, what if I get sick and I am not able to teach my child? There will always be the what ifs and the what if questions will make you worry and scared. But this is where your faith comes in.

Here are some scriptures for those who worry. Isaiah 41:10, "Fear not, for I am with you; Be not dismayed, for I am your God. I will strengthen you, Yes, I will help you, I will uphold you with My righteous right hand." I Peter 5:7 says, "Casting all your care upon Him, for He cares for you." Matthew 6:34, "Therefore do not worry about tomorrow, for tomorrow will worry about its own things. Sufficient for the day is its own trouble." John 14:1 says, "Let not your heart be troubled; you believe in God, believe also in Me. Lastly, Philippians 4:19 says, "And my God shall supply all of your needs according to His riches in glory by Christ Jesus."

Where God guides, He provides so we must really seek the Lord concerning our children and our homeschooling journey. When worry comes your way, that is an indicator to spend time with God. Remind yourself of the promises of God. "Don't worry, be happy!"

Writing

I KNOW THAT WE ARE DOING MORE TYPING AND TEXTING than actually writing these days, but writing is still a necessary skill. As a homeschooling parent you should be sure that your child learns to read and write well. I know that reading and writing go together; however, for the sake of this chapter, I will focus on the significance of writing.

Children start learning to write as early as pre-kindergarten and continue building upon their writing skills through high school. If they continue on to college, they will definitely build upon what they learned in high school throughout their years of college. It is so important for children to have a good foundation to build good writing skills. First, they start with letters then putting letters together to form words. Generally, children are learning to write their names first; then they move on to writing other short words.

If you start homeschooling your child during the beginning years between ages 3-5, you will have the pleasure of teaching your child how to read and write. You will be your child's primary teacher; therefore, you can make sure that your child develops a strong foundation in reading and writing. It is so important that a child learns to express himself in writing. Writing starts with children learning to write letters, words, sentences, paragraphs and then building up to essays. The essays eventually turn into papers and reports that students will have to write in high school and college.

Reading to your children and having them read books is a great way to help build a child's vocabulary as well as their writing skills. The important thing is not to give up on your child. Encourage them to keep reading and writing. Many of the schools have taken handwriting and cursive writing out of their curriculum. Since so much of our communication today is done electronically, many are losing the art of actually knowing how to write. As a homeschooling parent, you should be sure that your child knows how to write well.

Chapter Twenty-Four

THE X, Y, & Z PRINCIPLES

X-Ray

WE ALL KNOW THAT AN X-RAY IS A PICTURE TAKEN OF THE INSIDE OF YOUR body. It is a very helpful tool that allows us to see what can't be seen on the surface. Normally, doctors use x-rays to help them diagnose problems and to make decisions about your body. To x-ray something is to take the time to examine, investigate, inspect or carefully inquire about whatever you are doing. As a homeschooling parent you will need to x-ray the subject of homeschooling. Spend some time talking to those who have homeschooled and those who may be currently homeschooling. Ask questions, examine, investigate and even go and visit a homeschooling umbrella or a co-op where homeschooled children attend. The more that you x-ray the topic, the more information you will have to make your decision.

I also believe that the X-ray Principle applies to homeschooling because as a parent you will be able to x-ray your child. It's one thing to send your child to someone else to be educated but it is another thing for you to educate your own child. As you spend daily time teaching and raising your child on a one on one basis, you will be able to see past the surface of your child. You will see things that may not be visible on the outside. You will see the skills, gifts, talents and some valuable things that are inside your child.

When you start seeing some things you will need to encourage, speak a word of life and do everything that you can do to nurture and nourish the gifts that are inside. Know that God has given each of us a purpose and a reason to be on earth. Some of us will never find these treasures or have them nurtured because no one was able to see on the inside. As you homeschool, God will show you your child. He will give you X-ray vision and insight to see inside your child. Some of the things that you see may not all be good; you may see some things that you will need to work on. Perhaps things that your child was able to get away with in a traditional school setting are those that you would like to see done differently. When things are revealed that are not to your liking, you will know how to pray and ask God for guidance to correct. Having X-ray vision as a parent can be the very thing that helps to save your child's life or helps to drive you to do what needs to be done for your child.

The "Y" Principle
You

ALTHOUGH HOMESCHOOLING IS ABOUT EDUCATING YOUR CHILD in a non-traditional way and the focus is on your child, there needs to be a moment before you start where YOU (the parent) place the focus on YOU. I have intentionally highlighted the word YOU because I want to encourage YOU to focus on yourself for the moment. Ask yourself, "Am I willing to do this? Am I willing to sacrifice doing _____ to homeschool my child?" Homeschooling starts when parents decide they want to educate their child. When YOU think about it, shouldn't parents be their child's first teacher? From the time they are infants, we begin trying to teach them something. I remember nursing both of my children and one of the first things that I taught them was how to latch on to properly nurse without killing my nipple. Not only should parents be their child's first teacher, homeschooling should be something that every parent should do whether it is part-time or full-time. Often when a child does not know how to behave, people wonder and often ask the question. "Didn't your parents give you any home training?" Home is where your training begins and who normally does the training? "YOU" (the parent).

There is a lot of responsibility on the parent but with God's help, "YOU" can do it! However, "YOU" must be willing to do the work. YOU must take the necessary steps like doing the research to prepare and letting the state know that you are planning to homeschool your child. YOU must be sure that you have all the curriculum and the necessary supplies to homeschool your child. YOU must get daily teaching time with your child or be sure that someone else is teaching your child the necessary subjects. YOU must be sure that your child is getting everything that is needed at each grade level. YOU must be the best overseer of your child's education. What YOU don't know, YOU must ask; there are many people who have been there and done that and YOU also have the internet.

In closing the YOU principle, I want to encourage YOU to commit to doing what it takes to take care of YOU. Eat right, exercise, schedule time for YOU or time with family and friends. Do something that involves fun without your children. Feed yourself spiritually with the Word of God and be sure that YOU are good mentally, physically and emotionally. Make time for YOU and be committed to taking care of YOU. If YOU don't, it will be difficult to successfully take care of anyone else. Although homeschooling is demanding, YOU must make time to take care of yourself and to keep yourself together. YOU deserve it!

The "Z" Principle
Zebra

YOU MADE IT TO THE LAST PRINCIPLE OF THE BOOK, THE ZEBRA PRINCIPLE. If you have read my previous book, Marriage from A to Z, Principles for a Successful Marriage, you may remember this principle. The Zebra Principle is based on characteristics of the zebra. While studying the zebra, I learned that zebras are native to Africa and are closely related to donkeys and horses.

However, they are very distinctive because of their bold black and white stripes. The key thing about the zebra is that each zebra is unique. Zebras come with different stripes and patterns. Therefore, no two zebras are exactly the same.

Just as each zebra is unique and no two zebras are the same, no two homeschooling families are the same. There may be several homeschooling families but each will choose to do it differently. Just as each child, parent and everyone's home is different, each homeschool will be different. What may work for one family may not work for another family. What one parent decides to teach her child may be different from what you may decide to teach your child. Two families may decide to teach the same subject but they may teach it two different ways. One child may be taking a course online with no books and another child is taking a class in person with books. One family may be signed up to homeschool under the state and another may home school under a homeschool umbrella. One child may not complete their homeschooling requirements until their senior year and another homeschooler may finish their eleventh-grade year. When a homeschooler finishes early, that could mean attending a community college their twelfth-grade year. Another homeschooler may need all the time that they can get to finish all the high school requirements. There are just so many factors that can be different from one homeschool family to the next. Therefore, there is no need to compare. Do your best for your child. Learn what is needed to educate your child and focus on doing everything that you can to be successful!

The last thing that I will say about the zebra is that each of them have some black stripes and some white stripes. The black stripes represent the dark/challenging days and the white stripes represent light/glorious days of homeschooling. The dark/challenging days are when you are tired, frustrated and perhaps feeling drained. It could also be that you are having some challenges with your child academically or even behavioral concerns. Maybe your patience is being tried and you are questioning yourself with why you decided to homeschool. The white stripes represent the days when everything is going well and you are happy that you decided to homeschool. You are seeing that your child is learning and grasping what is being taught. These are the days that make you want to continue homeschooling. Well, if you homeschool for any length of time, you will experience both, some black stripes and some white stripes. The black stripes should remind you that you can't do it alone, you need the help of Almighty God. Psalm 46:1 says; "God is our refuge and strength, a very present help in trouble." He is a very present help when you are homeschooling and need the strength to get through a challenging day. God will see you through so don't give up! God created family and He wants to be included in every part of it. So remember not to compare your child or your homeschool with another. Just as each zebra is beautifully unique, each child, family and homeschool is also beautifully unique.

Closing

I know that homeschooling is not for every family. It was a wonderful experience for our family, and I learned so much on the journey. Although we homeschooled my daughter longer than my son, I am so thankful that God gave me the opportunity to homeschool both of my children. The time that I was able to spend with them was priceless. I pray that the principles in this book are helpful and that more families are encouraged to consider homeschooling. I am a witness that homeschooling works and that you can homeschool successfully. Try it!

About the Author

CAROLYN TATEM IS AN AUTHOR, SPEAKER, EDUCATOR AND ORDAINED MINISTER. In addition to homeschooling, Carolyn has taught middle school, high school, night school and various classes for adults. Currently, she teaches middle school. She is the author of five books. For over 15 years, Carolyn has served as the Director of The Queen Esther Ministry, a ministry that specializes in training and discipling women at First Baptist Church of Glenarden in Maryland. Many have been changed through her ministry. She and her husband, William, are leaders in their church and have a passion for marriage and families. They have been married for 22 years and have 3 children.

For more information and speaking engagements, please contact the author at:

www.carolyntatem.com
Connect on Instagram at carolyn_tatem
Twitter: @carolyntatem
Blog: marriagefromatoz.org

Other Books by Carolyn Tatem

Marriage from A to Z
Principles for a Successful Marriage

Marriage from A to Z Study Guide
Workbook for Married Couples

Marriage from A to Z for Singles
Study Guide for Singles and those preparing for marriage

Embracing Excellence
31-Day Journey through Proverbs 31 – Devotional

FOREVER
publishing

www.ingramcontent.com/pod-product-compliance
Lightning Source LLC
Chambersburg PA
CBHW070610010526
44118CB00012B/1484